Leading From The Front

Vignettes Dramatically Depicting Episodes
Of War And Peace From The Perspective
Of A Combat-Seasoned Command
Sergeant Major

Command Sergeant Major Gretchen
Evans, U.S. Army (Ret.)

Forward By Erik Weihenmayer

4

Leading From The Front

2

This book is dedicated to all those who have served in uniform.

Contents

Forward

Erik Weihenmayer

Adventurer, author and speaker - the first blind person to reach the summit of Mount Everest and the Seven Summits, solo kayaked the Colorado River through the Grand Canyon and Co-Founder of No Barriers USA

As I was losing the last traces of sight right before my freshman year of high school, I could see just enough to press my face to the screen and watch TV. One of my last visual images was a show featuring Terry Fox, a Canadian who lost a leg to cancer as a teenager. As he lay in the hospital, watching other kids suffer and die around him, Terry made a bold decision, to run across Canada to raise money for cancer research. His journey covered thousands of painful miles, a marathon a day, on the primitive prosthetics of the era. Before Terry could complete his "Marathon of Hope," tragically he succumbed to cancer, but what I saw on his face as he ran, captivated my attention, and has directed my life ever since. Beneath the grimace of struggle and agony, there was a light that burned within him; facing my own tremendous struggle, I wondered if that light also burned inside of me.

I have now spent the better part of three decades trying to grow that light through my climbing expeditions to some of the highest mountains in the world and kayak adventures down some of the fiercest rivers. However more importantly, through my No Barriers movement, I've tried to seek out others who also fan that internal flame despite the ferocious storm that swirls around them. Gretchen Evans is one of those people. Just as many will struggle to associate blind and climber in the same breath, Gretchen and Command Sergeant Major don't exactly match up on paper. At first glance, Gretchen, at about 5 feet tall, with a slight build and soft southern drawl, wouldn't strike someone as a candidate to lead troops on the battlefield. But, she rose to the highest enlisted rank in the Army, a Command Sergeant Major, and not only oversaw but fought in heavy combat alongside the soldiers in her battalion.

While she may be unassuming in stature, it is her character in which leadership and command shine through. In her compelling story, Leading from the Front, Gretchen guides the reader through the delicate balance on the front line: authority and compassion, leadership and camaraderie, levity and loss.

In war there are no good outcomes, only damage control. Gretchen's memoir is a stoic but emotional recount of the thousand tiny cuts and a few major gashes that left her, like the Scarecrow in the Wizard of Oz that she likens herself to, shredded and in pieces. And by her own admission, the injury from the blast that deafened her is far less damaging than the insidious creeping fog of decades of trauma.

We will all live with wounds and barriers, many that will never fully heal or be overcome. Yet, it is the spirit with which we rise that Gretchen embodies. As she remarks, there is no "taking back bullets fired," but there is leaning in, opening our hearts, and performing a kind of alchemy:

harnessing our hardship to elevate and transform the world for the better.

About the Author

Gretchen Evans, a combat veteran, served 27 years and retired as a Command Sergeant Major (CSM). She led and trained service members of all branches worldwide in peacetime and combat. She held every enlisted rank in the U.S. Army from private to Command Sergeant Major and every position from squad leader to Corps Command Sergeant Major.

She is an avid runner, hiker and bicyclist.

She is involved in several veteran-centric organizations assisting veterans in navigating post-service life. Her passion is helping others, finding innovative and successful methods for healing, growth, and companioning the broken. Being wounded in war and diagnosed with a Traumatic Brain Injury and PTSD, she utilizes her personal experiences to journey with others.

Introduction

The Scarecrow

Scene 1

"We're off to see the wizard, the wonderful wizard of OZ. Because, because, because, because, because...because of the wonderful things he does."

Admit it, we all know that you sang that song in your head.

Dorothy, the Tin Man, the Lion, the Scarecrow, and little Toto too, were on the Yellow Brick Road and Emerald City was in sight. They have defeated the Wicked Witch of the West in her ruthless pursuit of destroying them, along with their dreams of going home, receiving a heart, a brain, and courage. Victory is just past the poppy fields, just down the road.

But their adversary, the witch, has one last weapon in her arsenal -- those mean ass monkeys that she deploys to prevent them from reaching the places where they believe their dreams and wishes will be fulfilled.

Just when they believe all is well in the world, one last final assault ensues. Those monkeys with their creepy hats swoop in, chanting loudly, separating, and scattering the group until they find what they identify is the weakest member of the group. That's how bullies operate. They go after the weakest link.

They pounce on the Scarecrow and begin ripping the stuffing out of his body throwing it in every direction. They toss it all up and down the Yellow Brick Road. Scarecrow's buddies try their best to shoo away the monkeys to no avail. In the end, the Scarecrow lies immobilized on the ground. He has been unstuffed, his straw scattered all around. He is powerless and vulnerable, unable to put himself back together. He has been ripped, left in tatters, emptied and then thrown about, and now lies in the road conquered.

After the assault and chaos that ensues, there is a subdued response when one is alone, quiet, stunned, in shock, with nothing left with which to respond. There are no longer any offensive weapons to be used. There is not even a defense. One is completely defenseless.

And then it hits you, we are no longer who we once were. Our substance has been altered. That which made us who we are is missing.

Lying defenseless on the ground, staring into space, helpless, sometimes hopeless, depleted, and spent. Time is elusive. It's as if it doesn't exist, even though the world continues. It's as if time has stopped completely.

All the while, Scarecrow's friends frantically run about grabbing his stuffing, doing their best to place it gently back into his body. He needs them; he cannot do it alone.

But good news awaits. Shortly thereafter, the Scarecrow can stand again. Emerald City gleams, beckoning them.

This is me. I am the Scarecrow.

Scene 2

"Can you tell me what it feels like?" queried the psychologist who was sitting squarely in front of me. Just minutes before, I had entered his office. I did not want to be there. I was unstuffed and I knew it.

Thankfully, he had done his homework. He had taken the time to read my military records *before* my arrival. Per protocol, I had been told during my intake that I would go through six weeks of counseling.

His first words to me were abrupt but profound. "I cannot unfuck 27 years of trauma, Sergeant Major, in six weeks. You are going to be with me for a while."

Indeed, I thought.

I had stuffing scattered in Grenada, Nicaragua, Honduras, El Salvador, Panama, Somalia, Kosovo, Bosnia, Iraq, Afghanistan, in my home, on my post, in my church. I was immobilized, defeated, and helpless to help myself. I needed to be put back together, if I had any chance of being whole again. I literally needed to be re-stuffed.

And so, it began when I received my hearing service-dog Aura from America's VetDogs. Aura became my ears and a replacement for my lost tribe. She gave me the confidence to resume life with meaning and drive. At my lowest point, her unequivocal love, devotion, and sense of duty saved my life in that moment of ultimate despair. To this day life is fuller and richer standing by my side.

Having survived giving up on life with the help of Aura, I then experienced another life-changing moment when a battle buddy of mine reached out and spoke of his experience with No Barriers USA. Having just come back from an expedition, he spoke of finding hope, connection, a team--"a rope team."

With little hope of being accepted into the No Barriers Warriors program, I sent in my application. I had anticipated a rejection due to the extent of my injuries and my recent diagnosis of Post-Traumatic Stress Disorder. Who would take a chance on me? Would anything help me? Could anything possibly help restore me? In my anguish, I wondered.

Much to my surprise, I was accepted! The healing environment provided by No Barriers was the space I needed to move forward. Before, during, and after No Barriers provided my group and me with avenues to replace hopelessness; not only with hope, but with a renewed passion for living life to the fullest! Confidence lost, now restored. A new team committed to supporting me and to one another...a new way of life... a life with No Barriers. Sitting around the campfire on the last night of my No Barriers expedition it was time to make a commitment towards my future. I pledged to write this book. As I looked into each of my fellow Warriors eyes as I made this pledge, I knew that I could not let them down or myself.

"With a little help from my friends," as the Beatles would sing, and countless mental health professionals, my family, hikes in the mountains, swims in the seas, miles and miles of running, oceans of tears, Aura, and No Barriers, I stand again.

My life story continues to evolve. And here, I stand.

I think about the men and women who died in combat.

I think about so many harrowing stories of service and sacrifice for our country, even to the point of giving everything one has -- their life -- in defense of this country. And here, I stand.

When God asked, Who will go? I responded, "Here I am Lord, send me." And by His mercy, I am still alive. And here, I stand.

And when I hear the National Anthem being played and memories flood my soul, I stand.

For those who read these words and get it, you understand. There are great days, good days, OK days, and crappy days, just like everyone else. But regardless of the adjective used to describe my days, here I am. I am still standing.

Standing means I'm still alive. It represents hope. We all need a purpose greater than ourselves. We all need to feel alive. We have all lost a part of us that needs to be put back in. We are all in need. People often see the visible wounds of war, but it's the invisible wounds of war that can be the most difficult and deadly.

That is what drives me. That is what gives me purpose and meaning.

With the same resolve I used to fight the enemy, I now find the exhausted, the broken, the "un-stuffed."

With relentless determination, I do what Scarecrow's friends did for him - what Aura and No Barriers did for me. I find ways to help people get their life back. I literally pick up the pieces and re-stuff others as best as I can. And I will not stand for anything less. This is now who I am. And here I stand.

1

PFC Weeks

His name was Private First Class (PFC) Cary Weeks. Everyone called him Cheeks Weeks because he had, well, large cheeks on both the upper and lower halves of his body. How he made it through Airborne School was beyond me, and I know I wasn't alone in that sentiment by any stretch of the imagination. PFC Cheeks was chubby, the slowest runner in the battalion, and plain old goofy. His looks and actions were the farthest thing imaginable from the typically chiseled and disciplined paratrooper. Truthfully, he was somewhat of an embarrassment to the battalion.

Many of the Soldiers in the unit teased him, and for the most part PFC Weeks took it all in good stride. I had heard about a few times when they had been harsher than acceptable, which prompted me, as the battalion Command Sergeant Major (CSM), to speak with his company First Sergeant. Each time the First Sergeant assured me that he had the situation under control; however, this First Sergeant was suspected of being an asshole himself. I decided that I would pay closer attention to what was happening with PFC Weeks. A little ribbing among Soldiers is normal, as peer pressure can certainly be a healthy motivator, but I needed to ensure that it didn't reach a critical level.

Every decent CSM has a mole in his or her unit, preferably more than one. It's a necessary evil because the CSM is so far removed from the daily goings on of the individual Soldiers. You must have a trusted agent to give you the real scoop and let you know when things get out of whack. It was from my mole that I had heard about the First Sergeant's proclivity toward assholedom. It was also from my mole that I heard about of one of the members of PFC Weeks' company subscribing him to at least five different porno magazines.

The magazines were addressed to PFC Weeks' unit mailbox. This was embarrassing for the young Soldier for several reasons. He was very shy, and the only male Soldier I knew in the battalion that was neither married, dating, or both, as did some.

The mailboxes at the battalion were very small so anything larger than a standard-sized letter was required to be picked up in person for security reasons. I was told that PFC Weeks had to go to the mailroom several times a week to pick up these porno magazines. I decided that I would pay the First Sergeant a visit as soon as we returned from a training exercise scheduled for the next week.

The 82nd Airborne Division, our division which is based out of Fort Bragg, North Carolina, mobilized to Fort Hood, Texas. Fort Hood is one of the largest land-mass military installations in the free world, and our large division needed a large training area. Fort Hood is home to the 1st Cavalry Division (1st CAV) and its more than 16,000 Soldiers. There has always been a robust, but healthy, rivalry between the 82nd and the 1st CAV. Both divisions have distinguished operational campaign histories. Then there's the leg versus paratrooper rivalry. A "leg" is what we call a Soldier who hasn't earned the Parachutist's Badge for successfully completing Airborne School.

The training exercise was rigorous, but went as planned. We returned from the North Fort Hood maneuver area to start preparations to return to Fort Bragg. A group of guys decided to go to the post club to celebrate. According to my most reliable mole, this is how the incident started:

My guys were seated at a table eating dinner, washing it down with a few beers. They had been pretty much keeping to themselves, chattering about the kinds of things Soldiers talk about when they've been in the field for a week. PFC Weeks got up and headed for the latrine. As he passed by the bar, a 1st CAV Soldier, sitting with some of his 1st CAV friends, says something to the effect of, "Only dumbasses jump out of airplanes and it looks like you might need two chutes to keep your fat ass in the sky."

Well, PFC Weeks, who was no stranger to being the butt of many jokes throughout his life, let the insult roll of his back and kept moving. When he returned the same way from the latrine, the same 1st CAV Soldier made another snide comment to Weeks then boldly directed something derogatory to the entire group. PFC Weeks sat back down without a word. The gauntlet had been laid down.

Knowing that alcohol and heated rivalries go about as well together as bleach and ammonia, I decided to bring my executive officer (XO) to the club to check on things. We spotted our guys, wandered over and joined them, completely unaware of the overtly mounting tensions.

Just as I sat down, the 1st CAV Soldier at the bar decided to run his mouth once again. "Oh, not only do you let fat people in your unit, but girls too!" Well, that was the straw that broke the proverbial camel's back. The next thing I know, a chair that one of my guys was sitting on had been launched toward the bar. It hit a couple of the 1st CAV guys and mayhem ensued. Drinks got tossed and broken glass was everywhere. More chairs got thrown while splintered wood littered the floor. A couple of ladies near the scene scattered; panicked screams added to the commotion. It was an all-out brawl.

At one point, I jumped on the back of some CAV guy, trying to wrestle him to the floor. I was pulled off by another and thrown to the floor. This didn't go unnoticed by my guys, escalating an already chaotic situation. When the military police (MP) arrived, the XO was in a chokehold, PFC Weeks was alongside his friends throwing punches like Rocky Balboa, and there were more than a few drops, streaks, and smears of bloody evidence.

The lot of us were brought to the MP station. We were separated, 82nd Soldiers in one cell, 1st CAV Soldiers in another. A medic was dispatched from the hospital to assess whether anyone needed more medical attention than standard first aid. All of my guys, including me, had at least one black eye and a busted lip. The 1st CAV guys looked worse. We sat in our cells waiting for our respective Commanders to come arrive.

Prior to my Commander arriving, the officer-in-charge (OIC) had the XO and me removed from the cell so that we could speak privately. He asked us how we wanted to handle the situation. As everyone knows, there are three sides to every story: ours, theirs, and the truth. I paused and thought about the question. I would deal with it matter-of-factly. It's one thing for a bunch of junior enlisted Soldiers to beat the hell out of each other at a bar, but it's a different matter all-altogether when they start beating on a CSM and an officer. Things were a bit more complicated on this one.

When my Commander finally arrived, he sought out the XO and me. "I thought you guys were going down there to make sure nothing happened?" he said.

"Well," I said, "that was certainly our intent sir, but they picked on PFC Weeks and when I walked in they called me a girl."

His response was unexpected. "Did we kick their asses?" he asked.

"Pretty much," I said.

Then he explained his plan. "OK, here is what we have to do. We should pay for half of the damage at the bar. I have to go and meet with the Fort Hood Garrison Commander and tell him we won't cause any more trouble while we're here for the next two days. And then I'll have to call back to brigade and make up something plausible." He finally breathed. "By the way, is everyone OK, and is that a black eye Sergeant Major?" Without even giving me a chance to answer, he stated, "Sheesh! I'll go sign the paperwork so we can get out of here."

As planned, I paid a visit to the Bravo Company's First Sergeant, PFC Weeks' First Sergeant, once we returned from Fort Hood. I arrived to my meeting a good fifteen minutes early so I decided to sit quietly on the hallway chair outside his office. I was certain he had no idea that I was there.

Not long after I sat down, the First Sergeant yelled from his office to the two privates across the hall in the orderly room. "Hey dickheads! Come in here and refill my humidifier."
The two Soldiers walked over to his office and one picked up the nearly empty plastic container and brought it to the male latrine. The chair on which I was sitting happened to be situated directly opposite the door to the male latrine.

I knew every building in the battalion inside and out, so I knew that the latrine was a small one-holer. The privates didn't maneuver themselves inside very efficiently so the door didn't close all the way. As I marveled at their lack of spatial awareness, I curiously watched, trying to understand why this seemingly simple task was a two-man job. Then, I got my answer.

One of the privates held the humidifier tank under the spout and the other turned on the faucet. I didn't hear any words or see any looks exchanged, but once the container was three-quarters full the private manning the faucet shut it off. Then they both unbuttoned their pants and took a turn peeing into the humidifier tank. Still without an audible word to each other or acknowledgment of my presence, they carried the full receptacle into the First Sergeant's office, replaced it on the unit, and scurried back to the orderly room.

A minute or so later, the First Sergeant stepped out of his office and saw me. "Sergeant Major, I didn't know you were already here. Come into my office."

Like hell, I thought. I responded, "You know First Sergeant, I need to postpone this meeting. Let's meet in my office this afternoon at 1400." As I was leaving, I leaned into the doorway of the orderly room and addressed the two Soldiers who had peed in the humidifier tank. "After 1400 today, the First Sergeant will be addressing you by your name and rank. Have a nice day."

It turned out that the fight at Fort Hood was one of the best things to happen to PFC Weeks. When strangers started picking on him, his unit – his guys – stood up for him. It didn't matter that he was awkward and slow. He was one of us and if you mess with one of us then you mess with all of us. As they say in Texas, "If you mess with the bull, you get the horns."

PFC Weeks' life got a little better in the ensuing weeks. I noticed that on the battalion runs, his company placed him in the middle so that they could help him. He seemed to interact more with other company Soldiers. And the porno magazines ultimately stopped, at least for him.

As for the Bravo Company First Sergeant, I relieved him of duty. He was an asshole, but worse, he was a terrible leader and a bad example of the NCO Corps. After that day, every time I saw those two young privates from the orderly room I couldn't help but smile. Life was good. Army Strong.

2

Wash Rack

In the Army, we call it "recovery," and I am
willing to bet it's not what comes to the average
civilian's mind when he or she hears that word.
There are no beach chairs or massages. A simple
way to explain recovery is that for every three days
a unit spends outside in a tactical field environment
it spends four days back in garrison (our home of
record) cleaning, repairing, restocking, and
resetting; at least that's the way it always felt. Our

efforts culminated in inspection after inspection to ensure we got everything just right. Depending on the scope of the field exercise, inspections could be held from platoon-level all the way to the division. Standing policy was to do our damndest to leave things better than we found them. This never came without significant effort. In a word, recovery could be tedious.

This particular recovery, we had come in from the field for the final time before the division's deployment. Although we weren't taking the vehicles and equipment that we trained with overseas, they still had to be recovered -- cleaned, maintained, and put back on line, "dress right dress," for the next unit to use. I asked General Hanks to drop me off at the wash rack while he attended a meeting. He agreed to swing by an hour later to pick me up for yet another meeting that we needed to attend together.

Upon arriving at the division wash rack and observing for a bit, I felt that things were running very smoothly. I had always enjoyed washing vehicles during my time as a junior Soldier so I decided that I was going to help. I removed my headgear and blouse and hung them on the nearest fence. This left me in a plain tan T-shirt from the waist up. Anything distinguishing my identity, Army-wise, was either sewn to my cap or still velcroed to my uniform top. I grabbed one of the large, powerful hoses and joined in with a group of my Soldiers washing caked-on mud and debris off a vehicle.

One of the Soldiers in this group was my driver, PFC Gamma. Suddenly, I got the idea that this would be a good time for some payback for driving me off a bridge on one dark night during field exercises, so I aimed my nozzle at Gamma's ankles. I must have caught him by surprise because the water nearly knocked him off his feet. Gamma, being young and playful, retaliated instantly by returning the favor. He targeted my ankles as well, which did in fact knock me off my feet and into puddles of run-off. The other Soldiers in our group saw the scene, and in less than 9 Airborne seconds we had ourselves a full-fledged water war with no less than 20 participants.

Those Soldiers not engaged in the shenanigans stopped what they were doing and became enthusiastic supporters of one makeshift team or another. They cheered loudly for someone to become the victors. As the war raged on, it developed into a strategic, take-no prisoners conflict. Soldiers were being thrashed about all over the wash rack. Plans were made to wrestle control of hoses away from opposing forces. Frontal attacks and flanking movements were being employed just as practiced in the field. It was an impressive display of warfighting tactics. Twenty minutes into this fiasco, with still no determined winner, a military police car came rolling into the wash rack with its bubble lights illuminated. The driver blasted his siren, which got our attention and stopped the chaos.

Shit, I thought.

A very serious military policeman (MP) in the rank of staff sergeant exited his vehicle and stomped over where most of us were gaggled. "Who's in charge here?" he yelled.

I glanced at one of the many signs posted all over the wash rack fences stating that it was against post policy to aim hoses at anything other than military vehicles; violators would be subject to the Uniform Code of Military Justice (or UCMJ); Commanders were to ensure wash rack protocol was observed; yada, yada, yada. I then took a deep breath knowing that this wasn't going to end well. Just as I was about to out myself to the cop, one of the platoon sergeants unexpectedly called out, "That would be me!" I gave the platoon sergeant what we affectionately called the "puppy look," you know the one with the head cocked to one side accompanied by a quizzical look, and remained silent. All the eyes at the wash rack were intently focused on either the platoon sergeant or me.

The MP pulled out his black book and fired off a series of questions. "What unit are you with? Who is your Commander? Who is your Command Sergeant Major?" The platoon sergeant calmly answered each question truthfully. I thought, *OK, this is good. We can walk away from this one without going to the slammer.* Unfortunately, it's never quite so simple. At the very moment I had found a small sense of relief in a line of questioning I found to be innocuous, I looked to my side and saw General Hanks' vehicle approaching. *Shit.*

The General's driver parked the vehicle next to the patrol car, which would have given General Hanks ample time to survey the scene as he cut the numerous strides needed to close on us. The MP immediately rendered the General a very smart salute then proceeded to explain the situation. I still believe he exaggerated a bit.

The MP acknowledged Sergeant First Class (SFC) Tucker as the senior person on the ground prior to the General's arrival. Then the General nodded his head and scanned the crowd. He looked directly at me. Recognition didn't appear to be instantaneous, and I'm not sure if it was due more to confusion or denial. I don't think he wanted to believe I was there, that he was trying to reconcile in his mind why, if I was there, was SFC Tucker claiming to be in charge. Maybe he was wondering if this soaking wet, disheveled, small person standing in a crowd of soaking wet Soldiers was really his Command Sergeant Major. He then gave me the "puppy look," which seemed to be going around a lot that day, but didn't say anything. I sensed he thought there had to be a very good explanation so he played along.

Wanting to impress the General, the MP suggested to that it might be in the unit's best interest to inform the Command Sergeant Major and let "him" take the necessary action since this was a non-commissioned officer run operation. The General looked the MP in the eye, and in a deadpan manner, said, "Sure. Great idea. I'll make sure she knows about it."

All I could think to myself was, *Shit. Did he really have to correct the MP's use of pronouns?*

"Oh," the MP responded, "Your unit is the one with the female Command Sergeant Major. I hear she is a real firecracker. I'm sure she will come unhinged when she hears about what went on here today."

General Hanks replied, "Yes, I am very sure she will be appalled by what has happened here today."

The looks on the younger Soldiers' faces seemed to be asking, Just what kind of unit are we in? A sentry swore at the General and is no worse for wear; a guy nearly drowned the CSM and is still her driver; the CSM started a water fight at the wash rack and a SFC lied about being in charge and the General played along. What is this?

But the older Soldiers, the seasoned troops, they knew exactly what had happened over the course of the last few months. We had become one. From this point forward, they knew what happens to one of us, happens to all of us. We would bear each other's burdens and joys, victories and defeats. We were each other's protectors, collaborators, and soon to truly be "battle buddies."

It wasn't that General Hanks and I condoned rule breaking. Rules had to be followed, but we policed our own, not some outsider. The previous months of deployment preparation did much more than refine our warfighting skills; it solidified our faith, trust, and loyalty to one another, the Army, and to our country. We were ready.

The General gave me a ride back to my quarters, so that I could secure a dry uniform prior to our meeting. On the way, he turned to me and said, "Smage, let's try to get on the plane in a few days without one of us getting court martialed first, OK?"

I smiled and responded to the "old man," "I'll do my best!"

3

HALT!

"Halt, motherfucker!" rang out in the darkness. Without a star in the sky and the moon hidden in thick cloud cover, it was the darkest of dark nights. The words pierced the veil before us with the same intensity of a flash of lightning striking entirely too close. Quite frankly, it scared the shit out of us.

After taking a moment to regain his composure, the General leaned over to me and whispered, "Is that the challenge?"

I had always made a habit of telling my Soldiers that I found eye rolling to be incredibly disrespectful, and that it would always elicit an ass chewing. Even if someone's words or actions warranted a good eye roll it was best not to do so. I was one to practice what I preached, so I refrained, even though it may have been the most justified of situations up to that point. Plus, I knew the General's response was 50 percent surprise and 50 percent exhaustion. We were less than a week away from deploying to Afghanistan and it had been a long, hard ramp up. It was to be my third and his second deployment to the country. This time the stakes were much higher. He was a Major General (MG) in charge of an Army Division and I was his Command Sergeant Major (CSM). We were both feeling the immense responsibly.

The next command we received was, "Advance to be recognized!"

Praise God, I thought as the correct command came out of the darkness. I knew the voice. I knew most of my troops' voices, but this one I knew quite well. It also explained why we absolutely didn't see Private First Class (PFC) Sharkley as we approached. He was as dark as the night.

The General and I complied by together taking three steps forward. At the same time, the clouds dispersed just enough that the moon, with all its brightness, put a spotlight on the two stars centered on his Kevlar helmet. PFC Sharkley stood with bandoliers crisscrossed on his chest, weapon at the ready and pointed at us, wide-eyed and open-mouthed.

"Shit, shit, shit!" he screamed.

I wanted to smile but that would have been inappropriate. Amazingly, PFC Sharkley got his shit together quickly enough to snap his M4 rifle out in front of him and perpendicular to the ground to render a proper salute while under arms. For a split second, I couldn't have been prouder. I thought it was impressive.

"Why don't you give the General the correct challenge word?" I gently suggested.

PFC Sharkley belted out, "Razor!"

Thank God. We both responded, "Sharp."

I took PFC Sharkley aside and gestured for him to lean forward so I could speak with him privately. He was well over six feet tall to my just barely north of five.

PFC Sharkley was a brand-new Soldier to our unit. He had just earned his Airborne wings a few weeks earlier and what he lacked in common sense he made up for in enthusiasm. I really liked this young man and strongly believe that you can teach

Soldiers how to do almost anything that the Army requires to be considered a decent Soldier: how to march, how to read a map, how to shoot. However, I think it's almost impossible to teach a Soldier how to really love his or her country, the Army and its traditions, and a battle buddy. They usually either came with an ingrained altruistic nature or not. PFC Sharkley had a sense of dedication, loyalty, and courage the size of Texas. He turned out to be one of my best Soldiers.

Nevertheless, I flashed PFC Sharkley my typical CSM look, which translated to *You better hope Jesus comes for you before I get a chance to deal with you*, then said, "Don't do that again PFC." It was all that needed to be said. When I turned away from him I smiled to myself, then looked at the General. The smile that was not reflected upon his lips was certainly evident in his eyes. It was hard to stay pissed at PFC Sharkley for any amount of time, but this was a good indicator of another very long night.

We departed a very freaked out PFC and returned to our vehicle. The General chuckled. "We have some characters, don't we Smage?"

Ain't that the truth and you don't even know the half of it, I thought.

At this point, I had already known General Hanks for many years. We first met during Operation Urgent Fury on 24 October, 1983. He was a young infantry Major and I was a young intelligence Sergeant. We were both assigned to the 82nd Airborne Division at the time and our initial introduction, which happened during the Grenada invasion, proved to be very memorable.

Throughout the duration of our careers, General Hanks and I crossed paths numerous times. We developed a deep mutual respect, yet I was still totally taken aback when he telephoned me six months earlier and asked me to be his CSM. It took balls for him to ask a female to be the top non-commissioned officer in the division, and even bigger ones knowing full well that his division was to deploy to Afghanistan. I was honored, shaken, and excited all at the same time.

"You've got to love troops, don't you Smage," the General said while the Humvee was rolling back toward the Tactical Operations Center (TOC).

"Yes sir, we do," I answered. "It's what we're given to keep evil at bay."

General Hanks looked at me over his shoulder. "By the way, did you get a new driver?"

"No sir, I'm keeping Gamma." He looked at me in surprise, and with good reason.

I was still relatively new to the unit and the Soldiers didn't yet know what kind of CSM I would be. I didn't know that just a week prior to running into the sentry that was PFC Sharkley, on another dark evening in the field, many of them would get their answer.

My unit was observing light and noise discipline, meaning that the young man at the wheel of my Humvee was driving without headlights, but was wearing night vision goggles, which are notoriously bad when it comes to depth perception. He approached a very narrow and wobbly bridge that spanned a creek. Unfortunately, PFC Gamma misjudged the width and got a tad too close to the edge. The Humvee tipped over, landing on its roof in three feet of water. The gunner, who was manning the turret, saw what was about to happen and had the foresight to safely bail out beforehand. I had been looking down at my map with my red lens flashlight and was surprised to find myself upside down and in water

The water was pouring in and I quickly looked at Gamma as I wondered what in the world had just happened. Honest to God I think he was in shock. He didn't respond to me as I yelled at him to unbuckle his seat belt. I reached across and did it for him then shoved him out of the Humvee. I unassed myself from the vehicle, waded around in waist deep water to the driver's side, and then grabbed PFC Gamma. As I pulled him up on the embankment to dry ground I heard my gunner broadcast on the division radio net, "Gamma just drove the CSM off a bridge! I think they've drowned! Medic! Medic!"

By the time PFC Gamma and I reached the top of the embankment a crowd had already gathered. There was a dead silence that is hard to

describe as anything but eerie as we walked toward
the gaggle of curious onlookers. Not knowing me
well, I believe the Soldiers were waiting for me to kill
Gamma on the spot.

A few moments later the General's vehicle
came to a skidding stop just short of the crowd. I
stood there, soaking wet in my full battle rattle,
mud caked to my calves, and debris covering my
uniform. Then the medics joined the fray yelling to
find out if I was all right. I held up my hand to
indicate that, in fact I was, and that they needed to
stop advancing toward me. The silence returned.

I truly believe that this was the defining
moment that demonstrated for these hardened,
heroic, and loyal Soldiers what kind of Division
CSM I would be. I pulled off my Kevlar, tucked it
under my arm against my side, and turned to PFC
Gamma. "Secure all our equipment. Get the vehicle
out. Take it to the wash rack and pick me up at the
TOC at 2100 hours. We have a busy night ahead of
us."

Gamma mustered a smile. "Sergeant Major,
am I still gonna drive for you?"

More than a hundred sets of eyes were on us. Not one person made a sound.

I calmly answered, "Of course PFC Gamma. Shit happens. We all make mistakes. I believe in second chances." I turned to General Hanks; he had tears in his eyes. "May I get a ride back to my tent sir?" I asked.

"You betcha, Smage!" he exaggerated.

There was no shame in those tears. They were tears of a man who understood and took seriously the responsibility of taking all these men and women to war knowing that, despite our best efforts, not all of them were certain to return. At that moment, I knew without doubt that together we would lead, protect, teach, and nurture every Soldier under our leadership with a firm hand and a compassionate heart. Everyone deserves a second chance.

4

Two US Airmen and the Ride of a Lifetime

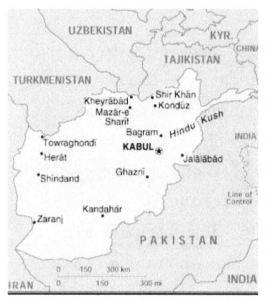

We were driving to Bagram that morning so that I could attend another useless meeting. The General had asked me to go in his place because he needed to be over at the US Embassy for yet another useless meeting there. Bagram is 47 kilometers (29.3 miles) from Kabul, but the road is dangerous for a variety of reasons. It runs geographically through land that belongs to

Warlords. But you never know which one is currently the new landlord as they kill each other off frequently. It also has unauthorized Afghan  checkpoints, which, by the way, we do not stop for under any circumstance. Sometimes they fire off a few rounds as we drive through, sometimes they wave. Another reason the drive was so dangerous was that Camp Eggers, our HQ, was in the middle of Kabul just down the street from the US Embassy, which meant you had to drive through the city to get to the main road, referred to as Jalalabad Road. I suspect every soldier that has driven down Jalalabad Road has a story to tell.

My security team and I would leave early that morning, right at daybreak so I would arrive in time for the useless meeting. We had been in country about three weeks and we were getting comfortable with each other. We were taking four armored Humvees with full combat load, just in case the drive turned ugly.

Gettin g through the city was treacherous that day. The roads were congested

as people were moving livestock and their products to sell in hopes of trying to eke out some sort of living in this dismal country. The Afghans I noticed had become less tolerant than before in my earlier deployments. They were not quite as happy to see this armed force in their country. Now that we had put President Karzai in charge and basically destroyed the terrorists training camps, I think most wanted us to go home. On occasion their frustration was demonstrated by throwing large rocks at our convoys as we drove through town. Although the rocks could hardly hurt us in our armored vehicles, there was something unnerving about people throwing rocks at you. It felt spiteful. It seemed that overall the Afghan people were ready for us to leave. They had grown tired of having us there, riding around in our military vehicles, imposing ourselves in their villages while we looked for bad guys. They wanted their lives to be normal again.

We arrived at Bagram safely. My team dropped me off for my meeting and they went over to the USO, which had just recently been named after one of our fallen Soldiers, the Pat Tillman USO. My meeting was intense and I had some unsettling news that I would be delivering to the General upon our return.

SFC Brayden, the NCOIC of my security detachment, approached me and said that there were two Airmen at the USO who need a ride to Camp Eggers and did I mind if we took them with us? The normal procedure was that everyone coming to Afghanistan flew into Bagram and whatever unit they were to report to would make arrangements to get them where they needed to go. The Airmen had called the Air Force entity at Camp Eggers but were told they could not come to get them until the next day. It seemed unnecessary for these young Airmen to have to sleep in the USO for a night waiting for their ride, so I said it was fine to come with us.

SFC Brayden put one of the Airmen in my vehicle with me. SFC Brayden always rode in my vehicle being the NCOIC so now we had five: the two of us, plus a driver, a gunner standing in the turret, and the Airman. The Airman sat in the back with me on the left side of the vehicle.

We drove out of the compound back onto Jalalabad Road. I was familiarizing myself with the key points of the brief presented, which held difficult news for my General, and formulating

recommendations for our response. The Airman sat quietly and very still, eyes forward. I am sure SFC Brayden told him that he was catching a ride with the Command Sergeant Major and therefore he was not to speak to me unless spoken to or something to that effect. It was probably more like, "Just shut the fuck up on the way to Eggers."

Focused on the brief, my head deep in the page, I was not concentrating on the drive back when at mile twelve, I was forced back to the present situation when we started receiving small

arms fire. *Shit*, I thought. I think most people think you just jump out of your vehicle and get on the ground and start shooting, but that is rarely the case. It is the gunner's responsibility because he has the best view to let us know from what direction and distance the attack is coming. We were waiting for his directions.

He yelled, "Three o'clock, 100 yards, exit left." SFC Brayden and my driver, CPL Gamma, were out of the vehicle immediately diving head first onto the ground. Brayden noticed that I was not out of the vehicle and I heard him yell, "Get out now Smage."

I was trying to get out, but the young Airman was glued to his seat. I had to crawl over to his seat and tell him, "You need to exit this vehicle quickly before they shoot a rocket at us." He did, but instead of staying low to the ground, using the profile of the vehicle for protection, he exited the vehicle like he would any other vehicle on any other day. He simply stepped out of the vehicle. Making an easy target for the enemy, he was shot immediately. I crawled out landing on top of him and we pulled him into the small gully on the side of the road that we were using for cover.

I immediately heard SFC Brayden on the radio giving our position and asking for a QRF (Quick Reaction Force) for reinforcements and indicating that he had precious cargo aboard, "Spitfire," which was my code name. We knew we had at least 20 minutes or so before the QRF arrived, so we maneuvered the troops to provide the best defense we could.

The Airman from my vehicle was dead. We then noticed that the other Airman was not returning fire. It rapidly became all too obvious that he did not have any ammo. *Fuck!*

The QRF came quickly, along with an Apache escort. They whisked me away while the Apache took care of the enemy.

When my team came back to Bagram, dropping the dead Airman off at mortuary affairs and then to retrieve me, they could sense I was very upset. I wanted to know how it came to be that I had two people in my convoy that did not have any ammo!

Here's what happened.

When the parent unit picks up their Soldiers, they bring ammo for their personnel and give them a brief on convoy procedures. My security team had made a grave error that cost a man his life. Because we do not normally pick up people from the USO, taking the Airmen was an unordinary act and they deviated from normal procedure. It is not their job to issue ammo or brief convoy procedures; their job is to get me safely from place to place. We had never carried another person in my convoy. Even the General and I did not ride together unless it was necessary. He had his team, and I had mine. It was never a good idea for us to be in the same convoy. If we did have to go together we were always in different vehicles. My guys were simply trying to do a nice thing by getting these two Airmen to their duty location, not thinking that they had not already been given ammo, nor needed to be briefed on convoy procedures.

We all sat around a circle as we debriefed the situation. There was plenty of blame for all of us. Top to bottom.

I could tell they felt awful and yet their mission is but one thing: to protect me at all cost. And that they did. In their mind, the Airman was a dumbass for getting out of the vehicle the way he did and not speaking up that he did not have any ammo and ask for some because we had plenty, believe me. I was so frustrated by the whole ordeal, but mostly with myself.

Why was I reading on one of the most dangerous roads in Afghanistan? Why did I not at least lean over and ask this Airman his name and shake his hand? Was what I was doing more important? He was probably scared shitless being in Afghanistan for the first time, much less finding himself in the CSM's vehicle. It would have only taken a minute to put him at ease, had I just taken the time to talk to him. I had failed at the one thing I said I would never do as a CSM. I put stuff over troops. I hated myself for this selfish act.

The drive back to Kabul was quiet. We all had failed at our jobs. Sorry was never enough, nor an accepted answer in the Army.

I could talk about the policy changes I made to ensure something like this never happened again and that was all well and good, but I will never forget that this young man died six hours after landing in Afghanistan. He never even unpacked his gear. I imagine he called home to tell someone he had made it safely into country. Then in a matter of hours, he would be on his way back home.

It is shit like this that keeps you up at night. That takes the flavor out of food and the joy out of just about everything. Shit like this makes holidays unbearable, casual conversations intolerable. Shit like this makes you weary of friendships, frightened of love, and unable to look in mirrors to see the person you have become.

Sooner or later shit like this has you sitting in a chair trying to explain to a professional why you don't like to drive anymore, or take passengers in your car. Why going through heavy traffic accelerates your heartbeat. Crowds become menacing to you, debris on the side of road reeks of danger. Shit like this has you question repeatedly, every person you meet, as to whether they are friend or foe. Intimacy becomes almost impossible with anyone who does not wear a uniform.

Shit like this makes you wonder if you will ever be able to say, "I have a new battle buddy, a friend, someone to call on the worst of days but also on the best of days."

Shit like this is unrelenting. It lingers forever.

5

House

"Kill everyone in the house," were the orders. Intelligence, supposedly, had been watching the house for several days. Three mid-level Al-Qaeda leaders were reportedly all in the same house at the same time, in a small village in the eastern part of Afghanistan. Like most villages in Afghanistan, it consisted of twenty to thirty very primitive houses, no electricity, open sewer system, and a well in the middle of the village that provided water for everyone. This village had a nine-foot mud wall built around the houses. It is rare to see women in an Afghan village out and about. If you do, they are accompanied by at least one man and they are in burkas.

We received the order to go, after confirming that the three men had entered the house. We had to act quickly and we set out immediately. We landed about 5 miles from the village and walked the rest of the way.

The plan was to go into the village on foot at night with a squad size element. We were armed with M4s, grenades, and night vision goggles. We would accomplish our mission and then be extracted by helicopter a half a kilometer from the village at a prearranged rally point. The plan was to surround the house, which consisted of one big room, begin the assault, first with hand grenades and then enter the house after the blast. There were two windows in this house. It was a structure made of dried mud and thatch. There were black cloths hanging over the windows making it impossible to see inside the house. Two of my men went to each window and were to toss in fragmentation grenades simultaneously, which are very effective in confined spaces. Then we would kick in the wood door and kill any of the surviving men.

We approached the house, tossed the

grenades, kicked in the door, and through the green tinted view of our NVGs realized that there were women and children in the house as well. The women were on one side of the small room curled up together with small children lying in between them. There were three women and four children, but we did not know that then. The body count came after. Based upon the intel information, we proceeded as if only men were in the house. We were not expecting any women or children to be present. We were dazed. We could not believe that we had just harmed these women and children. All the children appeared dead. One woman moved and one of the squad members shot her. I think it was instinct that caused him to shoot. I believe had we had a second to think, to process what had just happened, he would not have fired his weapon. At the very same time, without

even waiting to see or hear if any of the men were still alive, several of the squad members began firing at the three men. When we knew for sure they were dead, we headed quickly to the rally point breaking up into two groups and taking two different routes in case we were pursued.

When I got back to the Tactical Operations Center (TOC), I questioned how it could be that there were women and children in this house that supposedly had been under surveillance for several days? The answer: Women who are still nursing their children are forbidden to leave the house during this time. Their meals and needs are met by other women of the village. Therefore, the intelligence report stated that it saw women coming and going from the house bringing food, but that they always left before dark.

I do not know what else to say about this event other than all of us felt awful for what happened that night. There is no taking back bullets fired, no way to make up for what happened. A couple of my guys really took it hard. The killing of innocent people, especially women and children, does not set well with men of honor.

For me, it was another military operation that once again did not go exactly as planned. The killing of the women and children was not part of the plan; it was not done with malice or intent. It just happened. There is no effective way to place blame or anger in these situations. It just sits there in your inner soul and on quiet nights or lonely days, the image of those women and children huddled together on the dirt floor of that small house fills the mind's eye with crystal clarity, like a photograph. Sometimes the sight of a woman walking down the street holding an infant or walking with a toddler brings this image to mind. Sometimes walking into a dark room reminds me of that night.

I do know that I was not the direct cause of death for those women and children, but that does little to erase the image or change the fact that it did happen. The sorrow and shame remain.

6

The Milk Truck

It was not my finest day by military standards, but in retrospect I think this event revealed just how much I loved my Soldiers and how seriously I took my duties as a Command Sergeant Major (CSM) to heart.

A CSM is a unique rank: You are to be the advocate of the troops, the voice of reason to those above and below you in pay grade. I remember upon graduation from the Sergeant Majors Academy the words spoken to us at our final gathering, "You better be able to part the Red Sea because that is what is expected of you." I took this challenge seriously.

It was early in the days of the war in Afghanistan and we were still establishing secure and functioning Military Supply Routes (MSRs). It was a challenge to get the necessary logistics to our troops in a country that was completely landlocked, had no infrastructure, and was still very dangerous.

Simultaneously while combating insurgents, we had to negotiate with the Warlords who held control of the land across which we needed safe  passage and had to build adequate roads over which we had move our supplies. Negotiations with the Warlords required some compromise on both ends. Sometimes it went something like this: "I will not burn down your poppy fields if you will tell your men not to engage us on this route." Since we were not as concerned with their main crop, this was a good deal for us. Unfortunately, Warlords changed frequently due to endless internal disputes, often resolved by some sort of gruesome death of one Warlord, necessitating constant renegotiation. These were not treaties like we formed at the United Nations; they were in most cases simply a handshake shared over tea and lamb.

The scuttlebutt had gotten to me that the troops were longing for real milk. It may seem  unusual for milk to be so important in a war-torn country where attacks on our compounds were constant and those roaming the caves and harsh landscape were engaging the enemy continuously. Still, my Army was made up of mostly men between the ages of 21 and 24, and fresh milk was important to them. I needed to deliver. The powdered stuff just was not cutting it anymore.

As we all know milk needs to be refrigerated. This, in and of itself, caused some logistical issues. Electricity was sparse in the country, even on our own postage stamp-sized compounds. We were running off generators in most cases. But my G4 (logistics) guys had found a way to get a refrigerated truck flown in that could self-refrigerate for several hours. Just enough time for them to get it safely to the compound where we would be able to hook it up to a generator.

The day had come. The truck arrived at Bagram AFB where we had sent a security detail to escort the truck to the compound. There was great anticipation for the arrival of the truck. I think the troops had requested hordes of chocolate syrup bottles from family and friends from the States to make the arrival even more, well, sweet.

The security detail took charge of the truck

 upon arrival and began the trip to our location. Along the way, they encountered an attack from hostiles and under intense

fire had to abandon the truck. Now safe, they hurried back to camp. As the gates flew open we were all excitedly anticipating the large milk truck. Instead, the only thing we saw was the escort vehicles. I quickly learned what had happened.

Although I comprehended what I was told, the situation still made no sense to me. Why would they take our milk truck if it was not plugged into electricity? In a few hours, the thousands of gallons of milk would spoil quickly in the intense heat of Afghanistan. I knew these nomadic troublemakers surely did not have any electricity. What was the point? Plus, I had recently negotiated the safe passage of this route? *Damn it, I was mad.*

Normal standing procedures require that we sit down and write a five-paragraph operation's order – often referred to as an "O" plan -- detailing where we would go and how we would retrieve the truck. But to do so would have simply taken too long. Instead, I felt like Popeye: "I've had all I can take and I cannot take any more." So, I launched an ad hoc rescue mission. My words at the front gate went something like this, "I'm going to get the milk truck. Who's with me?"

I did not lack for volunteers. We mounted up in our armored vehicles, I grabbed my translator who I could tell really wanted to sit this one out, and took two Apache helicopters with me. Off we went to rescue the milk truck.

The security force took us to where the truck had been captured. There we found a few lingering "shepherds" armed with AK-47s standing around, their camels loaded down with their worldly belongings on their backs. We encircled them with our vehicles and mounted MK-19s at the ready. The Apaches were hovering above and I requested my translator to ask the men where the milk truck had gone. At first, there was the Sergeant Schultz "I know nothing" response. I then looked them straight in the eye and stated emphatically that if they did not cough up the milk truck I was going to shoot their camels on the spot and burn down their poppy fields.

My translator gave me the "Really, this is what you want me to tell them?" look. My guess is he gave them the direct quote because they instantly started conversing. As I was talking to the nomads I was pointing to their camels as I threatened to send them to camel heaven. Each time I pointed,

 the Apache pilots looked in that direction. Because their guns are maneuvered by the direction of their head movements, the guns would turn toward wherever I was pointing. This was unnerving not only to the hostile nomads, but to my own troops that had dismounted to provide security for me as they took steps back each time I pointed. Also, camels can spit slime about five yards and nobody likes to get slimed by a camel.

Finally, one of the hostile nomads made his way over a sand-covered hill and in about 15 minutes our precious milk truck appeared. We secured the truck and returned to the camp without incident.

The troops were happily singing the song from the Cosby show, "Mom is great, now we can eat our cake, the milk is here, let's all cheer," or something to that effect. Meanwhile word had gotten out that I went rogue, and even perhaps had a mental breakdown and launched an unauthorized mission to rescue ... "a milk truck." My General was waiting for me when I returned to the TOC.

"Um, Sergeant Major, did you go outside the wire recently?" the General asked.

"Yes, indeed Sir, I did," I replied. I wanted to say, "That is a fact, Jack," but I knew I might be on thin ice here.

"I did not see a convoy request or operations order, perhaps it is still with the G3?"

I replied, "Sir, you know I did not file an order nor request convoy approval or coordinate shit, they took the damn milk truck, and I just went to get it back. Go have a glass of milk, Sir."

His look was of concern. "Sergeant Major, was there like any gunfire exchanged or injuries or damage to equipment on this, um, mission?"

"Nope," I replied.

"And is that our troops out there singing, "Mom is great, now we can eat our cake?" he asked.

"Indeed," I said.

"Sergeant Major, when was your last day off?"

"That would be 9/10/2001, Sir."

"How does four days in Qatar sound to you, Smage?"

I looked him in the eye and softly stated, "It really wasn't about the damn truck Sir. You see, I know you think that it was risky to go out and get the truck, and perhaps a waste of expensive assets.Tten vehicles, forty men, and two Apaches. But you see, this is how it starts. First it is a milk truck, then it is an ammo truck, and it just goes on from there. There will be no stopping them. Plus, the route was negotiated for safe passage and they attacked our convoy. We had to nip this breach of agreed negotiations shit immediately. I had promised the troops that they would have milk. I gave my word. If you want to write up a counseling report stating I'm 'batshit crazy,' go ahead Sir. I understand. Will that be all, Sir?"

He nodded and walked back to his office. I headed over to the mess tent, took a long hard look at the gleaming silver milk truck and my troops drinking chocolate milk and eating cake. Life was good.

Come to think of it, I never did get that four-day pass to Qatar.

7

<u>Milk Dud</u>

The Army has countless rules. We call them regulations. This should not surprise anyone who has ever read a book or watched television. So, while we have an enormous amount of field manuals (FM), pamphlets (PAM), and unit standard operating procedures (SOPs) instructing us in how to win our nation's wars, there are a large number of regulations intended to uphold the "good order and discipline" of the fighting force. For example, FM 3-21.8, *The Infantry Rifle Platoon and Squad*, is an infantryman's key tactical manual, while Army

Regulation (AR) 670-1, *Wear and Appearance of Army Uniforms and Insignia,* outlines... well... exactly what the title suggests.

One might think that common sense would eliminate the need to formally institutionalize some regulations, such as tying your combat boots tightly to your feet or buckling the chinstrap on your helmet. Other regulations sometimes leave me scratching my head wondering what exactly happened that compelled a ranking person to establish said rule – the obligatory, reactive "knee-jerk" regulations. I compare these to the McDonald's incident when a person was burned by hot coffee and now paper cups come with a printed warning that "Contents may be hot." Seriously?

I mention the differences between the types of rules, because leaders are regularly required to make decisions concerning enforcement of regulations. In my experience, the good leaders understood the difference between those never to be compromised and those with built in flexibility. Soldiers, after all, are only human and the human psyche can only take so much.

Acquiring pets in Afghanistan was highly discouraged; in fact, it was against Army regulation to have a pet while in country. There were several reasons for the rule, but the risk of contracting a disease was the one most often cited. It didn't stop many military members from picking up a stray dog or cat though. I even saw a pet goat or two during my tours in Afghanistan. There is a natural inclination to want to care for an animal in need, especially when your family is thousands of miles away, and you just want something to wrap your arms around and tell that everything is going to be OK. And so, it was about two months into my third trip to Afghanistan that I knew my guys had acquired a puppy.

They did a pretty good job of hiding him for a

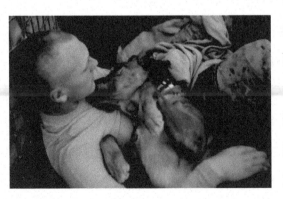

while, but when I started noticing bootlaces connected by knots in unusual places I became suspicious. Puppies chew and I knew that. When I called my Soldiers out about the puppy, they responded by handing him to me. He quickly ended up on our unofficial battle roster and I found myself ordering dog treats from the States. I then did what all good CSMs do and let my Commander know that "we" had a pet on the compound. The conversation went something like this:

> "Say sir, there is a unit over at the other compound and they have a pet puppy. This puppy is a great morale booster for the Soldiers and they have grown to love him. They have vaccinated him for rabies and all other diseases dogs can get. He sleeps with them in the hooch and they have arranged for quality dog food to be sent over from the States, housetrained him, and on occasion taken him out on patrol. Do you think the Commander over there should know about the pet puppy, and if so do you think the Commander should do something about it?" The General took a deep breath. He answered, "No, I don't think it's something the

Commander needs to know about as long as the Command Sergeant Major is on top of the situation." He then asked, "Does this puppy have a name?"

"Yeah, they call him Milk Dud because he got into the foot locker with all the snacks and ate a whole box of Milk Duds."

"What does he look like?" he queried.

"He's black and tan with really soft fur... um... from what I hear." I sheepishly stated.

"Oh. Well, is he going to get really big?" he asked.

"I don't think so. Medium-sized like a lab. I think." I responded.

"When he goes on patrol, where does he ride?" he again asked inquisitively.

"Well, last time he rode between the two seats in the back of my vehicle." *Shit.*

Three days later, the platoon sergeant was conducting a pre-combat check before we left on a mounted patrol for the day. I didn't normally go out on these types of patrols. The General discouraged me from going too frequently. While it was dangerous for everyone, it was especially dangerous for me as a high-ranking military female. The Taliban would covet making an example of a woman in their crusade against Western values. This particular day, the General admitted to me that he worried more than normal when I was out on patrol.

"I don't want to see you on CNN with a blindfold on and a gun to your head," he said. "But I know you need to be with your troops. Just be careful."

"We will as always, Sir," I assured him.

In our area of operations, I had established three patrols that ran 24 hours a day, seven days a week. One patrol rode less than a kilometer from our camp and one rode five kilometers out. The third rode somewhere in between. That day our route was to be the farthest from the perimeter on the edge of what we called the Red Zone. We made it very clear to the Afghan people that they were not to venture into the Red Zone unless they coordinated with us first.

There were five armored Humvees in our convoy, four of which carried Soldiers armed with M4 rifles and a gunner's turret mounted with a MK-19 Automatic Grenade Launcher that shot 40mm belt-fed rounds. My vehicle contained five personnel: my driver, an interpreter, a gunner, Milk Dud, and myself. We had been out about an hour when we spotted four men on foot within the Red Zone. As we approached, our vehicles fanned out and we set up so that the Afghan men were covered from all angles.

The patrol leader, the interpreter, another Soldier, and I dismounted our vehicles and advanced toward the four men. Milk Dud exited the vehicle as well, staying close to my side. We could see that they were armed with AK-47s, which was not unusual. As always, we proceeded with caution and stopped about five feet short of them. The Soldiers in the other vehicles took up positions behind the opened armored doors while the turret gunners locked their sights in the direction of the Afghan men; all weapons were at the ready.

The patrol leader had the interpreter ask the men why they were in the Red Zone. In the same breath, he wanted it communicated that they were to leave immediately.

We waited for one of the Afghani men to respond. To tell us why they had so blatantly breeched protocol, gone against common knowledge, which endangered themselves and others. All I heard was the shot. We all heard it. What I remember hearing even louder, and what I still hear to this day in my nightmares, was the collective gasp of my guys when we realized that one of the Afghans had shot Milk Dud in the throat. In the very next second, if it was even a second, the gunner in the vehicle closest to the four men opened up with his MK-19.

From where I was standing, I felt the rounds whiz by my head. The barrage nearly completely separated the men's torsos from their legs. Their blood splattered on my face. I felt "Milk Dud's" body weight drop on my right boot. There he laid, our beloved Milk Dud. As I took in what had just happened, I wanted to scream. *Why him? He was just a pup. He did nothing wrong; he's an innocent bystander in this war. Why didn't you shoot one of us? We are the enemy; your fight is with us. We are Soldiers meant to die on the battlefield, not him. There are rules, even in war. You don't fucking shoot things for no reason. What the fuck is wrong with people?*

I used all the strength I had to not fall to my knees, scoop Milk Dud into my arms, and cry. In that moment, I wanted to rail at the world. Every injustice I had witnessed to that point flooded my mind. The memories of every Soldier I'd seen killed, every funeral I'd attended, and every letter to a family I'd written, enveloped me in a way that left me gasping for breath. But this was neither the time nor the place for me to come completely unhinged. I had a responsibility to the precious, brave men standing around me.

We stood in silence for a minute, the smell of gunpowder and death permeating the air. My ears still ringing from the blast of the MK-19, I knelt down and picked Milk Dud up. *Motherfuckers. Why, why, why?* was all I remembered initially thinking.

I had a lump in my throat so large I couldn't swallow. Tears threatened viscously to fall from my eyes. *God, please no. Help me. I cannot... here... now.*

"Get back in your vehicles. Let's go," I said in a low, soft voice without looking at the others.

Knowing that the shots were most likely heard by the other patrols, I quickly got on the radio and transmitted a situation report about the contact. "Four enemy KIA, one friendly KIA. No need for reinforcements. Headed back. Out."

Not a word was said on the drive back to the compound. Milk Dud's lifeless body was draped between the back seats in my vehicle. His bandana with our unit patch sewn on the front was still around his neck and saturated in blood. We entered the front gate and put the vehicles back on line. No one exited.

Hearing that there had been one friendly KIA, General Hanks was there to meet the convoy, a grave look on his face. Before he could get a word out, I told him that Milk Dud had been shot. I thought he needed to know right then that it was not one of his Soldiers. Being the kind of General and person that he was, I could tell that he knew the loss we suffered that day was as devastating as if we had lost a Soldier.

Milk Dud represented all that was good to us in this God-forsaken place. He helped us maintain our humanity. We could show Milk Dud kindness and love without being accused of being soft. We cared for him like we did our children back home. We cuddled and hugged him; we made up songs about him. He was good. He allowed us to look at ourselves in the mirror and remember we were good despite the things we did. Milk Dud didn't judge our actions, our orders, our methods. He saw the good in us when we could no longer see it in ourselves. He forgave us when we could not forgive ourselves.

We unloaded our gear and each went back to our individual spaces. I had a private tent next to the General's that was constantly guarded by a Soldier. I walked up to the corporal. "You're dismissed for the day," I said to him.

"But Sergeant Major, there always should be someone here," he objected.

"Not today, Corporal. You're dismissed," I stated.

The young man reluctantly removed himself from my presence. I entered my hooch, flung my rucksack against the field desk, unholstered my weapon and threw it to the ground. I fell to my knees then flat upon the dusty ground and cried. I cried huge tears, alternating between heaving silently and screaming inwardly. The General, who normally asked permission before entering my tent, came in unannounced and sat on my cot. For a long time, he said nothing while I cried myself out. Finally, he rose, put his hand on my head gently and said, "Oh, Smage. I am so very sorry," and quietly walked out.

Later that day we buried Milk Dud behind our makeshift chapel. We threw in a small American flag, a dog tag from each of us present, and fifteen boxes of "Milk Duds". He was good to go. The Division Chaplain, a man thought very wise, said a short service, alluding to his belief that all dogs go to heaven, which was good because none of us was interested in going to heaven if Milk Dud wasn't going to be there.

Throughout the day I could see that my boys wanted revenge; Hell, I wanted it myself. We lost a part of our unit that day. It might sound ridiculous to those who have never experienced war, but what was taken from us that day was not just a dog. Our core had been shaken, our belief in humanity was in question, and our rules of engagement had been altered, at least in our own minds. The raging lion inside of most good warriors had been aroused and was waiting for an opportunity to be released.

I reckon that afternoon I became the most hated CSM in Afghanistan. I put all the Soldiers who were on that patrol with me on interior compound duty for the next couple of weeks. I was afraid they might let the rage they were feeling overpower their training and good judgment. I wanted to keep them safe until the pain subsided, until the tears fell less often, until we could all breathe again. We needed a reprieve. *"God help us"* I prayed. The Soldiers were pissed and very outspoken about my decision, but I didn't care. I knew what had to be done and unfortunately this wasn't the first time I had to subdue such rage.

8

Mission: CATch and Release

I was walking past his office, having just come in from a walkabout around the compound, when the General caught me right as I was walking into my office. "Sergeant Major, do we have a cat problem?" "Damnit" I thought to myself, "Cat problem, Sir, what do you mean?" as I kept an incredibly straight face.

Don't tell me, I could not win at poker in Vegas, I thought to myself.

"Well, I have just come back from my briefing at ISAF HQ and their General said that their compound has been invaded with cats," he replied. "Well Sir, ISAF is currently under

Command by the Italians, if you were a cat would you eat at the Italian/European compound or here where we serve MREs most of the time?"

Clearly at this point I had given him a plausible question as I could tell he was contemplating his response, "Well I never thought about it that way, Sergeant Major. That makes perfect sense."

"Indeed," I responded happily, mistakenly thinking we were done with these questions.

Unfortunately, the General was not so quick to give up on things.

"But, it really has gotten bad in the last month or so," he added.

Clearly, we weren't done with the issue of cats, so I quickly retorted, "Well Sir, I assume word has gotten around the cat community about where the best food is to be had, don't you think?"

This was a leading question designed to push him over the threshold of cat logic. At that point, he looked at me as if I had three heads. I could tell he did not want to think that cats communicated about where the best food was to be had.

Thankfully, he could not come up with a better answer. He had bigger fish to fry and moved on to more important topics, thank God.

I went to my office, closed the door and took a minute to ponder if I might be a tad crazy. I knew there was a reason why we did not have a "cat problem," but since I was trained in the art and science of intelligence, I wasn't going to quickly let on as to why that might be.

We had been in country about a month. General Hanks was the Combined Forces Commander-Afghanistan which means he was the senior military General in country and in charge of the entire theatre. I was his Command Sergeant Major. We and our staff were located at Camp Eggers, Kabul, Afghanistan, not even two blocks from ISAF headquarters and several embassies. So, it didn't make sense to the General why they would have a significant cat problem while we didn't. Even small details such as this are noticed by Generals.

Camp Eggers was a small compound, crowded with no way to expand because we were in the city of Kabul. Simply put, we were landlocked. Security was very tight since we had no less than seven General officers on the compound from various services and other countries. Our overall maintenance and logistical support was provided by the company we will call ABC. We had very few junior Soldiers on the compound. Most of them were on security forces, positioned in high towers and at our gates. It took a special ID card to enter our gates or an escort.

Upon arrival at Camp Eggers, it only took a quick assessment that at any given time our camp could be overrun if the enemy chose to assemble a massive attack. We had nowhere to go, surrounded by buildings and houses. The evacuation plan was to whisk away key personnel to the American Embassy, if possible, and the rest of the occupants would stand fast and fight, hopefully getting reinforcements from ISAF.

As I walked about that first week I noticed these small cages all over the compound. I inquired about them with the ABC guys and they told me they were cat traps. Apparently stray cats would enter our compound looking for food. I had noticed a few wandering cats about, but they seemed harmless to me. ABC informed me that if they did not trap the cats we would be overrun with them and they carried diseases as well as being a nuisance. I asked what they did with the cats after they caught them and without hesitation they told me they put them in bags and tossed them in the river. *What*, I thought. Surely there was a better option, but I was here to fight a war and our cat issue was way down on my priority list. Still, I found myself lying awake at night thinking about the cats. War does this to you.

I am not what you would call a "cat person," but this being my fourth combat tour in as many years, I had seen enough killing of people and animals to last me a lifetime. I could not get the merciless killing of cats out of my mind.

I called CPL Gamma into my office one day. Gamma had been with me a long time. He was a trusted agent, plus he was very resourceful. He no longer drove for me as I had a whole platoon of infantry that made up my Personal Security Detachment, but Gamma and I had a bond.

"Gamma, do you like cats?" I asked.

"Well, I do not dislike them." he said.

"Have you noticed the cat traps all over the compound? Have you wondered what happens to the cats ABC captures?" I asked.

"Not really Sergeant Major." he said.

I then responded, "Have you watched many movies about the mafia, Gamma?" This is when I got the puppy look.   He tilted his head and with a slight pause and inquisitive illumination,

"You mean they throw them in the river?" At this point, things were becoming much clearer in his mind.

"Yup," I said.

Trained in the art and science of strategic war, it was time to use our abilities for good. Gamma and I devised a plan. We had intel

that the traps were emptied every morning right at daybreak. So, our plan was to release the cats before them. We would put them into burlap bags, sneak out of the compound (go outside the wire) with the cats in the bags and make our way over to the ISAF compound where they would be safe. Earlier Gamma and I had found the one place over their wall where we could safely release the cats. We would then scurry back to our compound and enter the gate where Gamma had recruited one of the Soldiers to let us in quietly and not log our entrance or exit. I hope Gamma found a career worthy of his talents post military life.

The first few nights it was just Gamma and me. We were violating all kinds of rules, not to mention common sense. I could not even think of what might happen had we been caught by the bad guys. Me being apprehended or captured would have been a really big deal. Just the other day after a security briefing, where the General and I were told there was a bounty on our heads, the General told me to be extra careful when I left the compound.

"Sergeant Major, I don't have to tell you what would happen if they got you. I don't want to see you begging for your life on CNN," he said.

My response was terse, "I will never beg for my life on CNN Sir."

Still, I got what he was saying and on every occasion, I left the compound ensuring that I had my Personal Security Detachment (PSD) with me and a decoy convoy. This cat saving mission was personal and private. Somehow killing these cats, just because they were hungry, went against my moral thermometer. It bothered me in a way I still cannot fully explain. There was enough killing going around, let's not just kill out of convenience. That was too much. There was something subhuman about killing cats and kittens who were just hungry. It ate at me.

After about a week of the cat rescue mission Gamma and I realized we needed help. It was just a matter of time before something bad would happen outside the wire. So, I asked Gamma to discreetly find other vigilantes. I made it clear that they had to keep their mouths shut and understand that if we got caught by the bad guys or even our guys, either way, we were screwed.

So, it became a nightly ritual for the now four of us to rescue the cats. We looked forward to the mission. It made us feel good. In our small way, we could restore some of our moral code that had been chipped away and violated by war.

A year later when it was time for us to leave, I asked the new Sergeant Major to visit with me in my office. It was there that I told him about the cat mission. At first, I think he thought, just like I did, that I had a streak of crazy going on. Then, I could tell, he got it. This was not his first rodeo either.

I don't know if the cat mission continued or not. But these days I think about my cat rescue mission, and it always brings a smile to my face.

9

'Twas the Night Before Christmas

The night before Christmas my Soldiers and I stopped for the evening after spending the last week climbing up the rugged mountains of Afghanistan. Our mission was to rid the mountainside of the enemy that had been attacking some of our Forward Operating Bases and local friendly Afghan villages.

Cold, hungry and exhausted, we found a suitable staging point and sent out our observation and listening post Soldiers while the rest of us were to bed down for a couple hours before it was our turn to pull our shift. We huddled close with our backs to the mountain trying to stay warm. During this operation, a reporter from the Associated Press was with us.

This night as we settled in he pulled from his rucksack a satellite phone. He excitedly said to us all, "Hey, I have about fifteen minutes of life left on my phone, would one of you like to call home? It is Christmas Eve."

He handed the phone to the Soldier sitting closest to him. The Soldier took the phone in his hands looked at it for a couple of seconds and said, "I'd really like to call home, but Corporal Reed's wife is expecting their first child, I think he should call home."

He then handed the phone to the Corporal who held it in his hand a second and said, "No, I think Sergeant Weeks should call home, his mother is in the hospital, very ill, and not expected to live much longer."

The phone passed from Soldier to Soldier until it was returned to the reporter.

After a few minutes, as the battle-fatigued Soldiers finally began to sleep, the reporter came over to me and said, "Sergeant Major, where do you get Soldiers like this?"

My answer was short, "Soldiers like this come from America." What was unusual to the reporter was common to me: Soldiers putting others before themselves, loving their country, placing honor, duty, country and freedom above all else.

<u>10</u>

<u>FUBAR</u> Operation

It was mid-March and I remember distinctly

 the nip in the air that spring morning . Snow was still settled on some of the higher peaks but it no longer blanketed them and the valley below. The change in seasons was very much welcomed. It was the proverbial light at the end of the tunnel, signifying the coming end to our unit's current deployment to Afghanistan. We were in the home stretch – the last thirty days before unassing the area of operations (AO) and returning to Fort Bragg. I could almost smell the fresh baked apple pie.

Winter's end and spring's beginning, at least in calendar terms, had been one of the most brutal thus far for Operation Enduring Freedom. Our unit was in the process of finalizing the details of the battle handoff with the unit replacing us. It was standard procedure to "right-seat" the incoming unit so that they could learn the specifics of the area and its people from the Soldiers previously on the ground. Soldiers from the outgoing unit would usually spend time with their counterpart from the incoming unit. The idea is to "pass the baton" with limited disruption and maximized retention of knowledge prior to the formal Transfer of Authority.

As we assisted the new unit get settled, Al Qaeda had established a stronghold near the Pakistani border. They had placed it on the side of a mountain and were using its connected network of caves to move about freely. Within days, the activity in the area reached critical level and the terrorists' actions were becoming more brazen. They assaulted several local Afghan villages in the area as well as some of our Forward Operating Bases (FOB). This shit had to stop.

The call was made, and the command issued, to execute an assault of our own on the stronghold. In terms of manpower, we combined three platoons of Alpha Company from our unit and three platoons from a company of the unit replacing us to form a quasi-task force. Both companies would be led by their respective chains of command. In all, we would be putting around 200 troops on the ground, a more than adequate number given the previous evening's intelligence report: 100 estimated enemy with small arms, mortars, a grenade launcher, and an RPG.

In terms of the plan, since the terrain would not facilitate any vehicles and there was little to no cover or concealment, the task force would be flown

in via Chinook helicopters, advance up the mountainside, engage the enemy, clear the caves, and dispose of all weapons caches and ammunition. It was a straightforward plan, success partially riding on how close those Chinooks could get us to where we needed to be. There was no chance that we would have the element of surprise on our side; it was a daytime operation and we would be approaching in five rather large, rather loud troop transports. Surprise was never the point. We hoped that with a menacing enough show of force, they would choose this day not to fight. Perhaps even allow any civilians in the area time to leave without incident.

As the task force waited at the landing zone for the choppers to arrive, every Soldier took a knee. The previous night I had gone over the operations order to ensure I knew all the details of the mission. Then I went over it again, and then again, and then again. I memorized each platoon's objective, the order of march, the rally points, and the contingencies should alternate plans be needed. All the details that went into a well-developed operations order were covered. We would outnumber and outgun them. I was satisfied that it

was a good plan. I went over it again. My
concentration broke when a young Soldier with a
beautiful tenor voice began to sing. It went like this:

Up in the morning, out of the rack
Greeted at dawn with an early attack
First Sergeant rushed me off to chow
But I don't need it anyhow

Hail o' hail o' Infantry
Queen of Battle follow me
An Airborne Ranger's life for me
O' nothing in this world is free

From a big bird in the sky
All will jump and some will die
Off to battle, we will go
To live or die, hell I don't know

Hail o' hail o' Infantry
Queen of Battle follow me
An Airborne Ranger's life for me

O' nothing in this world is free

Early at night it's drizzling rain
I am hit and feel no pain
But in my heart, I have no fear
Because my Ranger God is here

Hail o' hail o' Infantry
Queen of Battle follow me
An Airborne Ranger's life for me
O' nothing in this world is free

The mortars and artillery
The screaming bursts around me
Jagged shrapnel on the fly
Kills my buddy, makes me cry

Hail o' hail o' Infantry
Queen of Battle follow me
An Airborne Ranger's life for me
O' nothing in this world is free

The group softly echoed each of the young Soldier's lines. Solemnity permeated the air. Those of us who had previously seen battle knew this was much more than a song. It was a story, a story that held the truths of days past, present, and future. We were confident, willing, and ready for the chance to do that which we had been trained to do. We were Soldiers. We trained to fight. Vowing to protect and defend those who cannot protect and defend themselves and to free the oppressed.

The helicopters approached, kicking up all kinds of sand and small rocks. It was go time. I looked around at the Soldiers closest to me. I would accompany 1st Platoon, Alpha Company (A1). As we prepared to board, the company Commander grabbed each one of his Soldiers by the hand, pulled them to their feet, and looked them square in the eye. We all bowed our heads to avoid the swirling debris and walked single file, one foot in front of the other, toward the birds and what destiny might bring that day.

I was on the first Chinook with A1. An interpreter, photographer, and three members of my personal security detachment: SFC Brayden, SSG Adams, and SGT Riccio accompanied us. These guys traveled with me always. I was particularly close with SFC Brayden. He had been with me in Afghanistan from Day One. SFC Brayden was my Spades partner when a group of us would get together in the evenings to play. We were terrible partners, both too big of risk-takers, so we seldom won. He was the one that always rode in my vehicle and the first to react to dangerous situations. It was love, but not romantic love. I don't know a word that properly encapsulates this love. It was neither spoken nor outwardly expressed in any way other than in the acts of our Soldierly duties. If what they say about the eyes being the window to the soul is true, then he and I had seen each other's. SFC Brayden was not my friend, my brother, or lover, but something more than any one of those things and more than all of them combined.

Lots of thoughts go through your mind as you mentally prepare yourself for battle. I am convinced that Soldiers have their own rituals and mantras that enable them to have courage. The courage to  face what they know might be a fierce battle where friends or perhaps they may die. Some pray. Others laugh and joke. Some carry a good luck charm. Others sit silently. For me, in that moment, I looked around the webbed bench seats of that chopper at the faces of each of my Soldiers. I thought to myself that there was no other place I would have rather been. It's hard to understand, maybe even harder to admit, especially to oneself, the contentment, but mostly, the pure joy felt of going into battle with your men. It sounds harsh, I know. It makes you wonder what kind of person you really are. That's not to say I didn't feel a longing to be home with my daughter and loved ones. There is a balance that must be struck to avoid tearing your soul, justifying your actions, suppressing your guilt, understanding you can't be in two places at once. I wasn't torn that day. I was in Afghanistan fighting a war. I wanted to be with these men.

One of the long-held traditions of the 82nd Airborne Corps is that when going into battle, the

first feet to touch the ground are those of the Commander and the Command Sergeant Major. So, when the chopper's skids got close enough, the Commander and I jumped, followed by 30-plus well-armed and eager paratroopers. It was A1's job to lead the task force up the mountain. Alpha Company's other platoons were charged with protecting the rear. The other company's platoon was to secure the flanks.

Approximately thirty minutes prior to our estimated arrival at the landing zone, our artillery battery had begun peppering the mountain. We were trying to discourage the enemy from hanging around. It became apparent about a third of the way up the steep rocky terrain that even the 155mm shells hadn't dampened Al Qaeda's resolve to maintain this stronghold; that's when we started taking small arms fire.

Bullets seemed to come from all directions. Front. Back. Both sides. This caused the platoon to disperse quickly and irregularly. I felt encircled. We attempted to re-consolidate as much as possible but it was proving impossible with the number of rounds coming our way. Then the worst happened. Nine Soldiers, the interpreter, the photographer, my security detail and I were completely separated from the rest of the platoon. A large group of Al Qaeda closed in from behind us and between the other platoons, effectively cutting us off from all other friendly forces on the mountainside. We weren't encircled as previously thought, but the fifteen of us had only one direction we could go: up.

It's hard to explain what exactly happened to the task force over the next few hours. I can only describe the events that unfolded before my own eyes. I had a radio and could hear all the traffic that was being relayed. Time and again, radio operators stepped over each other to broadcast over the net. The messages became mixed. There's no way to cogently explain what goes on in the midst of a battle that you don't witness. There are too many variables. No one expects a plan to go exactly the way it's written and briefed, but there is always hope that a decently calculated and well-executed operation will end in success. This current operation went what is termed FUBAR really quick. For those not familiar with what it stands for – Fucked Up Beyond All Repair. I didn't even have time to be pissed off about it. My guys and I were in deep trouble.

We bounded as quickly as possible up the steep terrain. The enemy pursued tenaciously. There was little to no vegetation to use as concealment; however, some of us were lucky enough to reach large boulders scattered across the rugged rock face for cover. The hailstorm of bullets didn't cease. Within the first ten minutes, three of my guys were hit.

The group stopped to render as much medical aid as the situation would allow. I jettisoned my rucksack knowing full well I wasn't going to need it that day. It had become quite obvious that I was either getting off the mountain today or not at all. My guys provided suppressive fire while I crawled on my belly to the nearest injured Soldier to assess his injuries.

I didn't know the Soldiers name and he didn't have a nametape on his flak jacket. He was curled up in the fetal position, pain searing his facial features. I looked him up and down. He had taken several rounds in both legs, one punching a gaping hole through the front of one thigh. And while I wasn't sure, I sensed from the amount of blood that he had been hit in the back below his body armor as well. I removed a syringe from his first aid pouch and injected him with morphine to subdue the pain. I also hoped it would reduce his heart rate to buy him some time until 2nd Platoon, who most likely had a medic with them, could give suitable aid. I told him I would come back for him and I meant it when I said it. Although I didn't know how I would do it while we were on the run from such a dogged pursuit. He thanked me.

I believe in situations like this, when a Soldier sustains a mortal wound, the wisest tactical decision is to take the weapon and ammunition to increase our firepower and prevent the enemy from using them against us. But in my mind, I couldn't just leave this man on the side of the mountain without any way to defend what life he had left. I wanted him to die as a Soldier dies – fighting to the death and leaving this world with honor.

I scratched and clawed my way over to the other two Soldiers. I knew neither. Both were grievously wounded. I administered each the contents of his morphine injector and reassured them we would return as soon as we could. Even then, as much as I wanted to believe those words, I knew in my heart that it was unlikely I would see any of them alive again. Their wounds were critical, but if possible, I would keep my word and come back for them. They knew I would too. I shook each one's hand, lingering and not wanting to let go. These days I'm not much of a hand-shaker. I find it to be a more intimate gesture than a hug. I crawled back to the others' location and gave the order to move on. Turning my back and continuing up the mountain was one of the hardest moments of my life. I dared not look back. The bullets continued to chase us.

In that moment, I wrestled with my decision to leave those men. Could we make a stand here and hold off the enemy until 2nd Platoon arrived? I had no cover and was short on ammo. What if it was SFC Brayden, SSG Adams, or SGT Riccio on the ground dying? Would I stay and fight? Did I decide to leave these men because they were unknown to me? I don't know for sure. I will never know. I swore to love all my troops equally, no favorites. The decision I made that day, in that moment, still haunts me.

Second Platoon was hot on the enemy's heels but was also fighting on their flanks as well. The further they pushed the enemy up the mountain, the faster my group had to move to avoid being overrun. Three to four at a time we leapfrogged up the slope. One group would move while the others provide suppressive fire. I knew that we would soon run out of real estate, so I started looking for a strategic place to make a last stand.

I radioed headquarters and requested Apache Gunship helicopter support. The thought was that they could back off the pursing enemy, but the reality was that friendly and enemy troops were so intermingled on that mountainside that it was too risky to fire into a crowd. It was pure chaos. Smoke accumulated and thickened and the gunfire was so loud I couldn't hear the Soldiers shouting next to me. I was bombarded by noise, yet could hear my own heartbeat. I had to close myself off to the overstimulation for just a second and think.

Then the thought pummeled me as if I was a boxer who had failed to keep her hands up to protect her head. I couldn't be taken captive on this mountain. As a female, I was lower than dog shit to these people, this enemy. As the highest-ranking non-commissioned officer in the division... Well, it didn't really matter. I was still female and still dogshit. I thought about what I might do should I be nabbed and I recalled a conversation my security guys and I had previously. We had come away in agreement that it wasn't in the US Army's or my best interest to ever be taken alive.

So here I am in the middle of this heinous carnage going over my options if capture was imminent. Should I take my own life? Should I ask one of my Soldiers to kill me? How about a kamikaze action that would most assuredly get me killed? I finally settled on a plan. It may seem morbid, but these kinds of decisions need to be made in advance so that one has the resolve to carry them out. I decided against asking one of my men to kill me since it would put him at risk for a court-martial. No, I would charge the enemy and hope that the ones who had closed on me first could shoot well enough to deliver a fatal hit. If that failed, I would do it myself. Decision made.

I put those thoughts aside and refocused on the entire situation. It was playing out in front of me like a broken VCR. The only button that seemed to work was the fast-forward. I decided the only possible way to salvage this clusterfuck was to order 2nd Platoon to stop pursuing the enemy up the mountain. In fact, they needed to back off entirely so that the Apaches could fire without hitting any friendly troops. I knew if this didn't work the situation would be worse than before. 2nd Platoon would never be able to catch up to the enemy before they overran us.

Directions to fall back were radioed to 2nd Platoon and we continued our ascent. Within moments of each other, all three of my security detail guys were hit. SFC Brayden was the worst. He had at least three gunshot wounds to his legs. SSG Adams was hit in his right arm and shoulder. SGT Riccio took a round in his side where there is a gap in the body armor. SFC Brayden and SGT

Riccio couldn't walk without assistance. Of the 15 of us who had been separated, and since the photographer and interpreter didn't have weapons, I was down to seven Soldiers still capable of fighting. Shit.

Second Platoon moved a half kilometer or so down the mountain. Once they radioed headquarters that they were at a safe distance, the Apaches seemed to appear out of nowhere. The scene was ear shattering as the gunships wreaked havoc on the Al Qaeda combatants. Smoke, fire, rocks, dirt, and metal shrapnel flew everywhere. We took cover as best we could, lying as flat as human bodies can possible lay behind the tallest cluster of rocks we could find. When the Apaches ceased fire, we started to move again. The air support stopped most of the enemy, but it didn't stop all of them. We continued taking fire up the mountain, all the way to the top.

The summit had an old lookout point probably left over from the Soviet-Afghan war. When we reached it, I took a moment to assess the situation. I looked over the ledge on the downward side. It was extremely steep and there was no way we were getting down it. I also knew that the group didn't have the strength to drag the wounded much longer. We could go no further. My decision was made. This 20-by-20-foot concrete pad would bear witness to our last stand. I radioed our position then steadied myself alongside my Soldiers and behind the sights of my weapon.

Then, out of nowhere, two Apaches and a Chinook materialized into my periphery. I had been given no heads up – no warning – no inkling, that they were en route. The Apaches ran interference as the Chinook hovered into position and then sat its butt on the pad. The ramp dropped and we loaded the wounded as fast as we could. I stepped off that mountain and into the safety of the metal hulking beast. I stared at its tailgate as it closed, too exhausted to sit.

I moved nearer to where SFC Brayden had been placed and took a knee next to him. A medic was attending his wounds. It wasn't good. He had lost a lot of blood from the badly torn flesh that left gaping holes in his body. I sat on the chopper floor and took SFC Brayden's hand in my own. His lips parted, I could tell he wanted to say something. I dipped my head close to his and in a voice, that was nothing more than a whisper, he said, "Save my spot at the Spades table, OK."

I said nothing in return. I only shut down. I no longer heard the whirl of the Chinook's blades or the roar of its engines. I no longer heard the organized prattle of the medics or the flight crew. It was complete, dead silence. I felt my heart slice. It was like a surgeon was dragging a number 10 blade across it center mass without an anesthetic. The pain was unbearable. I felt intensely lonely. I felt abandoned. In that moment, I had nothing and I wanted only to lie next to him and die right along with him. All sense of time and space left me.

At landing, SFC Brayden, SSG Adams, and SGT Riccio were immediately transferred from the Chinook to a medevac Blackhawk. I followed the crew to the other bird and made sure my three guys were loaded correctly. By the way, I hate those fucking helicopters.

Once the Blackhawk lifted off I walked over to the Chinook pilot to express my appreciation for the rescue. He shocked the hell out of me when he said, "Sergeant Major, we had been listening to the fight all morning on the net. We were pulling for you and your guys to make it to the top. All and all, it was a successful operation. The mission was accomplished." I looked at him incredulously as he looked straight at me. "You done really good. Everyone else is on their way back too."

I walked away without uttering a word. "Mission accomplished, my ass," I thought. A young Soldier caught up with me and relayed the message that I was wanted in the Tactical Operations Center. Of course I was. I had a brief conversation with my General via satellite phone. I remember the anxiousness in his voice, but I have no idea what I said to him in return. He informed me that my helicopter would pick me up and bring me back to headquarters the next day.

I went to find a quiet space. The same Soldier who pointed me in the direction of the TOC followed me and then handed me an MRE (Meal Ready to

Eat). "It's lunchtime Sergeant Major," he said to me. I looked at my watch. *Holy shit, it was only noon.* I was sure that we had spent days, not hours, on that mountain. Hell, it felt like a lifetime. The Soldier began to walk away when I asked him to sit with me. He agreed and I was glad.

I asked the Soldier about his background, his Army career thus far. When we finished our conversation over lunch we stood. He extended his hand to me as a thank you for eating with him. I reluctantly took it. It was the first time I had shaken the hand of someone other than my men who were left on the side of that mountain that day. Human connection means something. His hand was warm and strong. I looked him in the eyes and saw youth, hope, tenderness, and life. Then I looked at my uniform. Through the tears I saw only dust, dirt, and blood. The dichotomy of our current state was the epitome of our Army experience.

The following day I was notified that SFC Brayden died the previous night at Bagram Airfield. SSG Adams and SGT Riccio were airlifted to Landstuhl, Germany. They would survive their wounds, and for that I was grateful, but I wasn't so sure I would survive my broken heart. I didn't have long to dwell. The days didn't stop. The world keeps turning, even when you feel like you've physically left it. In the *Wizard of Oz*, the Tin Man braves the Wicked Witch of the West because he so desperately wants a heart. He obviously never considered the possibility that one day he would feel it shatter.

Later in the week, I was awarded the Bronze Star Medal with a "V" device for valor. Valor, what does that mean? According to the dictionary you can substitute every synonym for heroism in the English language. Truth be told, I may have exhibited courage, bravery, gallantry, etc., but what I really had that day was the unwavering desire and duty to get my men off

that God forsaken mountain. It really was that
simple.

     Hail o' hail o' Infantry

    Queen of Battle follow me

11

Running in the Rain

The General leaned his head and shoulders into my office, his feet still firmly planted on the other side of the door's threshold. "May I come in Sergeant Major?" he asked. Technically, he was already in, but I respected his attempt to provide me the illusion of choice in the matter, a choice not due to rank, but I could tell in this case, need.

"Sure sir. Come on in," I said.

He walked to the front of my desk and in a low, soft voice, the kind that small children use when they know they've done something wrong, declared, "I've got troubles."

In most cases when he has troubles so do I, it's just the ways things work. "What did you do?" I responded without bothering to look up from the document I was reading.

"Why do you assume trouble is always my fault?" he bantered.

"Well, always is a strong word, but this is not my first rodeo with you – or other Generals. Besides, I would know if I had done something to cause trouble. It's a simple process of elimination." He gave me a stern look that I knew was meant to communicate his disapproval, but that I took as acceptance of my point.

The General began, "My wedding anniversary is

this week."

I got up from my desk and put my hand up like a traffic cop. "Hey, hey, hey. Stop right there." I paced the room for a moment. I was already sure that I didn't want to go where this conversation was going. "What does that have to do with me?" I wanted to know.

"Well you're a girl and all," he stammered.

"I am not! I am a Command Sergeant Major!" I refuted with my most dignified command voice.

"I know, I know. But still…"

"But still nothing! Don't call me a girl!" My hands were planted firmly on my hips by this point. "You don't refer to me as a girl to others, do you?"

"Simmer down Sergeant Major. You know what I mean...not a girl, but well... I am afraid to refer to you as anything but CSM."

"That's a start. We've made progress," I derisively replied.

The General pleaded, "Gretchen, please just listen."

"Oh, now we are on a first name basis, are we? I would never call you Dick."

"Well that's good, because I actually prefer Richard," he said without missing a beat.

"I know that. I'm just saying." He smiled a sly foxy smile for just a brief moment. I knew that exchanges like these were one of the reasons he liked having me around.

"Where were we?" he continued, a bit of frustration now evident in his tone.

"We – as in me – were reading a very important training document trying to keep our division on task for our upcoming deployment." I state matter-of-factly.

"Ok. Let me just throw out some ideas and you can just shake your head." I shook my head east and west before he even made the first suggestion and I made my position known.

"Sir, I really don't want to play this game and I do not think it is wise of me to suggest an anniversary present for your wife. I'm not really qualified."

"Really? That's the card you are going to play in my hour of need? I have never heard you say you weren't qualified to do anything in the ten years I've known you."

Well, he had me there.

I thought for a second and countered his argument. "Well, if I suggest something and she doesn't like it she is going to be mad at me too. I'd rather have you mad than her sir. No offense, but quite frankly she scares the living hell out of me."

He rocked back on his heels. "I know, me too. That's why I'm asking for help." I saw his desperation mounting through the series of quirky expressions now cycling about his facial features. "We're about to leave and I'm going to miss the next one. And I have already missed so many. I want to make it special. I won't tell her you helped if she doesn't like it. It will be our secret."

"Oh, for the love of God! Really sir? When she doesn't like her present and throws you out on the street, you don't think you will break and throw me under the bus to save yourself?"

"I would think I would be braver than that."

"Yes sir, one would think," I replied dryly. "But on the chance, that you sing like a canary, I'd just assume stay out of the foxhole with you on this one. And by the way sir, do you know what a secret is?" The General narrowed his eyes and raised his brows; I'm sure wondering where I was going with my current line of thought. "A secret is information that only one person knows. When two people know it it's not considered a secret anymore."

"Geez, what is it with you intel types?"

"We just know that after the first fingernail is pulled, the secret usually gets spilled."

"Really Sergeant Major, you are being quite dramatic. I give you my word Sergeant Major, I will not crack."

I sat back down at my desk and motioned with my hand for him to do the same. The simple irony of the General sitting across from me in a seat usually reserved for the professional development of my young Soldiers was not lost on me. I relented. "I can't believe we are going to have this conversation sir, but go ahead. What are your suggestions?"

"Well, I'd like to get her a nice outfit."

Doubt immediately crept into my mind. "Have you bought her clothes before?"

"Yes," he answered.

"And how was that received?" I pressed.

"Awful."

"Well what the fuck makes you think you can do better this time? Have you been scanning fashion magazines on your off time?"

The General continued, "Don't be so negative Sergeant Major. With your help, I think I can do better." I sighed deeply. He continued, "What size would you say she is now? You know she has put on a little weight lately."

"Stop! Stop!" I shouted as I covered my ears and bolted around my desk to shut the door. "Don't say shit like that!"

"Like what?" he asked, shoulders shrugged and palms outstretched in front of him pointing towards the ceiling.

"I just don't want to know the details," I said. "Sir honestly, I have no idea and I would rather stick pins in my eyes than to guess what size your wife wears. Just the fact that we are discussing this makes me want to put a gun to my head."

"Please Smage, simmer down."

But I didn't simmer down.

"And another fact sir, I don't even know where you buy clothes like the kind your wife wears."

"Well I know her favorite shops. We could go there after duty hours tomorrow."

"Not happening!" In my mind, I'm now convinced that he's high on drug. "Are you taking drugs sir?"

With all seriousness he answered, "Of course not. Why would you ask such a silly question?"

"Because," I said, "You are acting like a lunatic right now."

"I'm desperate," he cried. *"Shit. Shit. Shit. He's desperate and now it has become my problem."*

I needed to get back to doing real work, but I could tell that he wasn't going to leave without a solution he found acceptable. So, I offered one, "Why can't you just give her a gift card to her favorite place? Throw in some flowers, candy... a new car... renovate the kitchen – and maybe, just maybe, your troubles will disappear."

The General got up from the chair. His expression was decidedly less worrisome than it had been when he first entered my office. "Well said Sergeant Major. I'll do just that." At that point, I thought we were finished but the General's feet remained firmly planted in my space. "On another note..."

"No other notes from you today buddy."

"No, seriously Sergeant Major, where do you go when it rains?" *"Well, that question came out of left field."*

I closed my eyes, lowered my head, and stopped breathing momentarily. The General went on, "Since we returned from our first deployment, every time it rains you either go for a run or run off to inspect something."

I let out a deep, audible breath then responded kindly, "Sir, the next time it rains you go with me and I will show you. Is that OK?"

"Sure," he said. The General started out the door then looked back over his shoulder. "Thanks for your help Sergeant Major."

"My pleasure Sir."

As luck would have it, bad luck that is, it rained two days later and I knew it was time to pay up on my offer. I really didn't mind sharing my secret with the General, that wasn't it. He had proven to be quite the officer; good to our troops, fought battles that needed to be fought, and had the good sense to let go of the ones that were unwinnable. You know, the whole "sometimes you need to lose a few battles to win the war belief." I figured that this was as good a time as any to answer the question he posed just two days prior, "Where do you go when it rains?"

Running or walking in the rain had been my respite from Hell for a very long time. It seemed to start off innocently enough. I just needed time away from, well, everyone and everything, and that was very difficult to come by. I needed this time to reflect and to grieve. The rain provided me a safe place, a chance to find some time alone. While most people ran to find shelter from the rain, I was drawn to it. It was my never-ending search for solace. On days like this one, I preferred to go for long, slow runs.

I changed out of my duty uniform and walked into the General's office. "Sir, it's raining. Change into PT gear and I will meet you out front in ten." He looked up to acknowledge that he'd heard me, bounced from his seat, and grabbed his gym bag without a word. We told our aides that we were going for a run and wanted to be left alone. I gave the nervous Soldiers a rough description of our route and an estimated time that we'd return.

The General and I started slowly. Hardly a word was spoken between us up until this point as we plodded along. About a mile from our headquarters building, on a long-deserted road, I initiated a stop. The rain continued to softly fall on us. He looked at me, still and quiet.

I reached into the tiny pocket sewn into the waistline of my Army PT shorts and produced a waterproof bag neatly folded into eighths. I handed it to the General, maintaining the silence between us. He unfolded the bag, broke the seal, and removed its contents, a single piece of paper. Though it was now protected from the elements, the paper was torn in some corners, tattered in others, and creased all over from being folded upon itself, countless times.

In the General's hands was a sheet that listed by day, month, and year, the name of every service member I had lost since the beginning of my military career. I say I lost. Sometimes these Soldiers were subordinates, sometimes peers, sometimes they were senior to me, but there they were. Some entries had personal notes in my sloppy handwriting next to their names. I had never shared this list with anyone previously.

The General examined the names and words on the page then glanced at me, glanced back at the paper, and then ceremoniously folded it back the way he found it. He placed it in the waterproof bag and handed both back to me.

"You see sir," I started, "I can come out in the rain and look at this list and well, you know, tears, rain, it all looks the same. I told myself that I would remember them forever, but I can't look at this list without the pain seeping through my eyes. The rain provides me, well, with a cover. I'm sorry I never told you before but I was concerned you might think I was weak."

He turned his back to me for a second, cleared his throat, and then faced me again. Even though it was raining, I could honestly see his tears mixing together with the drops from the sky. Who knew?

He said nothing. I said nothing. We ran back to the headquarters building. We cooled down for a bit with some stretches. Before we departed to our respective locker rooms I broke the silence when I asked, "Would you like to run with me again the next time it rains?"

"Yes," he muttered. "Sergeant Major, I don't know that I will ever be able to not run in the rain again."

"Yes," I said. "There is the rub."

Today, years after I have retired, I still run in the rain and I still carry that list with me. The last entry is 16 February. It lists the Soldiers lost from my last fight, the fight on the side of a mountain in Afghanistan. My own name is included.

Yes, I survived that fight, in body, but it doesn't change the fact that part of me died that day. It doesn't change the fact that some days I wish all of me had died if the truth of all twenty seven years of service were known.

I run in the rain just to remain sane.
My friends and buds lay in graves having no or little fame.
I know in my heart that we are not far apart.
I sway from feeling alive to feeling dead, for all those Soldiers have my heart.

12

Sleep and Dreams

"Do you have nightmares, Sergeant Major?" Gamma asked me this question a few months after returning from Afghanistan. "Yes," was my immediate answer, no sense lying to this young Soldier.

I find it hard to sleep, truth be told, I find it hard to want to sleep. Sleep summons dreams, nightmares and memories.

In my dreams, I change the truth, SFC Braydon doesn't die. I save the men I left on FUBAR mountain.

In my dreams, I make all the right decisions, I am flawless, we win all the battles. There are no stacked boots, rifles and helmets.

Photograph Credit

In my dreams, I'm not constantly trying to catch my breath, stop tears from flowing, my heart doesn't pound, I'm smiling.

One of my favorite dreams is when my Soldiers painted the cannon out front of another company's headquarters pink and added some texture to the tip. You get the picture. That shit was funny even though it cost me a serious ass chewing.

Another dream I really like is when I stand in front of the formation and play red light, green light with my troops. It was ridiculously immature and funny.

I dream of the sounds of feet hitting the pavement at dawn, singing cadence, running around the post, carrying the unit colors.

In my dreams, I can still hear my husband and daughter's voices and birds chirping.

One day while in Kabul, my sister sent me a bazillion red chili pepper Christmas lights. We hung them all around and just like on Chevy Chase's Christmas vacation movie we all stood still as a Soldier plugged them into an outlet, causing the generator to blow and knock out all the lights on the compound. Funny as hell, resulting in another ass chewing, but so worth it.

So, if sleep comes I rewrite history or dream of the best of times, only to be startled and awakened by truth. Dammit, I hate it when that happens.

I must stop now, I'm crying. Good night....

Epilogue

Resilience and Tenacity Forged in Adversity

I thought it best for the reader to have a glimpse into my formative years to best make sense of who I became and how I got to the top of the enlisted ranks. Every story of every Soldier is different. We all have a storied past. For some, the stories are more telling than others. For others, the military was easy compared to what they had endured in their youth. Whatever hand we were dealt in life, through trial and tribulation, we became a unit. We are family, we are whole and we are One.

We became -- Army Strong.

13

George and Merle

For a house run by a 21-year old, we quickly fell into what I would consider a normal routine. During the week, Kurt worked the oil fields, his days starting early and ending late. Eric and I got up and out to school promptly every morning of our own volition. On weekends, we did what normal families did, aside from the Friday night poker games with Kurt's friends from the oil fields. We cleaned the house, shopped for groceries, washed and folded laundry, and hosed down the car.

I became the check writer in the family and reconciled the bills every Sunday afternoon. We decided to open an account in all four of our names just in case (we had become believers in worst-case scenarios), but it fell to me to write the checks for the mortgage, utilities, insurance, and the other "surprises" that required payment. As we were on a tight budget, we cancelled cable television, the newspaper, and anything else we deemed nonessential.

Our parents had not planned to die so early or so quickly. In fact, they didn't plan for their departures at all.

George and Merle Watson were two of the most interesting people I had ever met. Both were strikingly beautiful. George was half English and half German. He was tall, blonde, blue-eyed, and perpetually tan. George grew up in rural Texas and when he was a teenager joined the Texas National Guard because the armory had the only pool table in town. Shortly after joining the Guard, he found himself a World War II pilot.

Merle was a petite debutante with dark brown hair, large hazel eyes, and a dazzling smile. Her daddy, my grandfather, was the judge in her hometown of Paris, Texas. She was the envy of every girl in her high school – prom queen (also known as football queen in Texas), cheerleader, editor of the school newspaper, and voted "Most likely to marry a handsome man," which she did.

When George returned from the war as a member of the Greatest Generation, he used the GI Bill to attend the University of Texas. During his sophomore year, George was elected to the Texas House of Representatives for Lamar County. It was then that he met Merle, who was studying journalism at UT. They courted under the pecan trees at the vast state capital building. Marriage came quickly and children soon followed.

Here was the rub.

While George and Merle were the epitome of this era's American couple – beautiful, patriotic, outgoing, and educated – they should never have had children. They were just not meant to be wholly responsible for others besides their beautiful selves. George and Merle loved to entertain and be entertained. They drank, smoked, and laughed to the extent that life could offer and they were madly in love with each other. All others were obscured in comparison. I can't imagine that George and Merle ever considered the gravity of raising children. I can only speculate that they devilishly enjoyed themselves a great deal of the time and that the consequences were four extra people in the household. Today's intolerant and overly sensationalized society would have considered them appalling parents – fodder for front-page headlines and the six o'clock news.

George and Merle saw Kurt, Dana, Eric, and me as four additional mouths to feed and it was their goal to make each of us as independent as possible, as fast as possible. They set few household rules. We had no curfews, school was optional, and we were free to openly express to them our discontent with our circumstances. I was six or so before I realized that all children didn't call their parents by their first names. It had never even occurred to me to call them Mom and Dad. They had names, George and Merle.

The first Christmas after their deaths, we set up the old 35mm movie projector in the living room. I remember seeing myself in a beautiful ruffled dress with black leather shoes pulling a wheeled cannon behind me. I toddled over to Merle, tugged on her skirt, and asked, "Where's George?"

George started handing out an allowance to each of us once we turned five. I don't remember what I did to earn it, but George conveniently instilled a method to get his money back. Every Sunday morning at the breakfast table he set up a gambling ring. He taught us how to bet on the NFL and it was winner take all for the day's lot of games. When we were a bit older he added point spreads to make it more interesting. I lost a lot of money until I turned seven and realized that I couldn't successfully win by betting on the teams with the prettiest uniforms. So, I started reading the sports page and heeding the predictions of the experts.

According to George, it was illegal for us to consult one another but sometimes Kurt, being the oldest, would subtly help the others pick our teams. If we won, Kurt required a cut. It didn't seem to bother George to take our money every Sunday. By the time anyone of us started to win with regularity, he died. *Shit.* To this day, we sometimes call each other on Sunday nights and confess that George would have gotten our money that day.

George was always bringing home very strange items, including animals. One time it was a tarantula in a glass mason jar that we of course named Charlotte. We used to let her roam the house freely, which freaked out most of our guests. Then there was the talking black bird. George hung her cage in the foyer and every time someone came in the front door she shrieked, "Close the damn door!" We named her Pepe and over the years she developed quite the vocabulary.

When we were all very young, George and Merle hired a part-time nanny for a couple of years. Her name was Carol and she was a beautiful, African-American woman. Carol was somehow able to navigate our strange household, mostly I think, by ignoring the aberrant happenings, but she was particularly uncomfortable when it came to cussing. For the most part, she overlooked this bad habit from her employers and their children, but she did not appreciate Pepe cussing at her every time she came through the door. One day she finally complained to George.

George knew that he couldn't easily find another person to live in our world for what he was willing to pay, so his course of action was to teach Pepe not to cuss at Carol. George's method for training included showing Pepe a photo of Carol while he repeated, "Good morning," over and over again. After a few weeks, Pepe caught on. From that point when Carol (and only Carol) came through our front door, Pepe greeted her with a robust, "Good morning. Close the damn door." George told Carol it was the best he could do. We were all impressed, less so Carol, but she conceded that her love for us was stronger than her distaste of Pepe's morning salutation.

Another unique aspect of our household, and one that I believe had a significant impact on my future self, was the Watson Trials. George was a lawyer and preferred to use the same tactics to root out criminals and deviants at home as he did in court. I remember the day when Merle came home from work and found all four of us sitting on the family room couch in birth order. In front of us was shattered glass scattered about the floor, the result of the large hole in the front window of our house. Mixed with the glass was a tennis ball, football, golf ball, and a nerf ball.

"What's going on?" Merle asked.

We all remained silent on orders from the prosecutor while he gathered the witnesses and jury for the upcoming trial.

Merle intercepted George in the hallway with an armful of stuffed animals and action figures, all about to be pressed into civic duty. She asked him what happened to the window.

I heard George say, "I don't know. They won't talk! I'm going to get to the truth now!"

Merle pleaded with him to hurry since they had dinner plans in an hour. George pecked her on the cheek, tapped her on the rear, and said, "Ok. I'll start with the baby."

Fortunately for us, an hour had passed between the time of the broken window and when George arrived home. We knew the drill and what had to be done. George always preferred to "get to the truth" through this process whenever the children were involved. He'd ask who was the guilty party and became despondent if we confessed too quickly. Confessions only happened if one of us had something better to do then have a trial...but today, today was different.

We had had time and were hoping to outsmart George. First, we tainted the crime scene with a plethora of balls on the family room floor. Second, we rehearsed with Eric, hoping to influence his testimony. He had just turned two and this was to be his first official Watson trial.

George started pacing in front of us, which signaled the start of the trial. True to his word he started with the baby. "Eric Karl Watson," he said. George always used our full names when addressing us to the court. Kurt reached over and pulled the pacifier out of Eric's mouth so he could defend himself properly.

"Where were you at 2:00 PM today?" he asked.

Merle stepped into the courtroom in a full slip and pearls. "George! Really you must get on with the trial, we have to be at the Jones' in half an hour."

Eric ignored Merle and answered George's question. "I weading a book in my bed."

"Ah," said George, "and what was this book about?"

"Wabbits," Eric said stoically.

George continued pacing. "Do you have any eye witnesses that can support this alibi?"

"Yes. Sister!" he said. George peered at me.

"Last question for you Eric Karl Watson, did you in fact break the front window of the house?"

Eric responded, "I did not," and promptly returned the pacifier to his mouth. The rest of us were so proud of Eric for successfully navigating his first appearance on the stand. George's frustration was palpable.

George pointed to Eric. "I'm not through with you. Stay put." He turned his attention to me. "Gretchen Georgeanna Watson. Did you break the front window?" I was a girl of few words. "I did not," I replied. Later, when I attended Counterintelligence School, I attributed my ability not to break under interrogation to George.

George moved on. "Dana Elaine Watson. Did you break the front window?"

Dana had already decided that she was going to be a lawyer like George. She stated, "I can neither confirm nor deny that I have any knowledge of said crime." George smiled and commented on the virtuousness of her answer.

Merle ducked into the room once more. "Really George, we must go."

"We haven't had all the testimony yet, nor reached a verdict. If I wait until later tonight all the suspects will be in bed. I'm teaching the children the importance of truthfulness, loyalty, and the court system," said George.

Merle looked directly at the oldest child. "Kurt, who broke the damn window?"

"I did," Kurt answered matter-of-factly. He knew better than to get between Merle and her dinner party.

Merle grabbed George by the hand and led him to the door. George turned his head over his shoulder and gave us a smile and a wink. "She could give Perry Mason hell."

Punishment was confinement to our bedrooms, as usual. Carol was our jailor and bore the burden of cleaning up the crime scene. Since we lived in a ranch style house and had become accustomed to periods of room restriction, we had rigged up a system of soup cans on strings that ran around the exterior of the house. This allowed us to pass clandestine notes. We even developed a special Watson code for our communications.

Someone would put a note in his or her respective can and then pull the string until the can arrived at the next window. If the note was for you, you took it, deciphered it, and responded. If not, you pulled the string so that the can moved to the next bedroom window. That night we did this for about an hour then I went to bed. The next morning, we each had a message in our can. It read, "I am so very proud of you guys. It took me an hour to break your new code. Damn good work. Love, George."

14

Texas Sun

The mid-afternoon west Texas sun was scorching hot. This should not surprise anyone who has ever been to Texas. This day it was personal, relentless, focused. My first day of ninth grade was complete. Now I was waiting in the uncovered bleachers of Mann Junior High's football stadium for my younger brother to finish practice. With the whole of my attention buried in an English assignment, the incessant beam of heat blasting the top of my head suddenly stopped. I looked up to praise the cloud providing the brief respite, but instead found Coach Villers, the head football coach at Mann Junior High, and my brother in front of me blotting out the sun. Their expressions were vastly different.

Coach stood in silence. He was the size of a refrigerator, and not one of those models with the freezer on top, the side-by-side kind. He was a kind man; I knew him well. For the past three summers he hired me to paint houses with him. I got paid $100 a house to climb a ladder and get to hard-to-reach places or slip my small frame into confined areas simply too difficult for him to reach. Sometimes, he tied a rope around my waist and hung me over the edge of a roof to get where the ladders couldn't even reach. One might say that his heart was as big as he was.

My brother too was silent, a deeply sad look on his face. I immediately thought that Coach was about to tell me he cut Eric from the team – a travesty of justice in my opinion. Eric was only in seventh grade but he had raw athletic talent. He was tall, lean, and handsome and had played football since the day he could walk. Every Christmas since he was three, he'd unwrapped a complete Dallas Cowboys uniform from under the tree. There were many mornings I watched him try to shove a spoonful of cereal through the faceguard of the helmet at the breakfast table. The uniform was replaced only at night with, of course, Cowboys pajamas.

Eric excelled at Pop Warner and honed his skills at countless football camps during summers. His dream, like most young boys in Texas, was to play for the Dallas Cowboys. At 13 years old, he was already six feet tall and could palm a regulation basketball in his gorilla-sized hands. The word around town was that he had a better than average shot at making it to the big stage.

About a minute of awkward silence passed then Coach blurted, "I have really good news! Eric has been selected as our starting quarterback!"

Well, I thought, *that is really good news.* So why was my brother doing his best futuristic Tony Romo – End of the 2006 NFC wild-card game – impression?

Coach continued, "He needs sweat bands, a mouth guard, and a jock strap. You can get them at the athletic store on Grape Street. Tell them he plays for the Falcons and they'll know what color bands to give you."

Shit. I immediately knew the cause of Eric's dejected visage.

That same morning, our oldest brother Kurt had given me ten bucks. He said it was for our school lunches for the week. He said it was all we had, but not to worry because the Social Security checks would be starting soon. He said that things were going to get better. Well, honestly, I didn't think they could get much worse.

Two weeks prior we had buried our mother. Six months prior we had buried our father. Kurt and my older sister, Dana, were away at college when both our parents got sick. Cancer killed them both, but I actually think my mom died of a broken heart.

Since Eric and I were minors, we needed a guardian. No one in our extended family stepped up to help. Foster care was mentioned but Kurt said, "Hell no!" He came home from school and petitioned the court to become our legal guardian. I remember the judge peering over his half-moon glasses, sitting on the tip of his nose, and with his piercing eyes, telling us that the minute he thought we were not "functioning" he would send in Child Protective Services to remove us and place us in foster care, and not necessarily together. I can't imagine that there were many people willing to take on two teenagers, even good ones.

Together we decided it was best that Dana stay in school and finish her degree. She was on her own but she was wicked smart. She was her class valedictorian and had a partial scholarship to Texas Tech University. She took as many credit hours as she could while working full time to expedite her graduation. We were in survival mode.

Coach Villers lingered after delivering the news. I know he sensed a problem. "Do you have a way to get to the store?" he asked.

"Yeah, I can drive," I answered, thinking back to that morning, pulling into the Mann Junior High parking lot and noticing that all the spaces were marked for teachers, staff, or visitors. We were none of the above. I politely asked one of the teachers in the lot about the location of student parking. She quickly pointed out that, "There is no student parking this is junior high. Junior high students don't drive."

Shit. Seemed to be my word of day.

Coach turned to leave then spun back around. "Do you have the money to buy the stuff?"

I said, "No sir, I don't."

"Come with me," he responded.

Eric and I piled into the front seat of Coach Villers' pickup truck. He drove to the athletic store on Grape Street and acquired the equipment Eric needed.

I wasn't sure whether Coach did this out of the kindness of his heart or because he was smart enough to know he needed Eric to win. (Eric led the Falcons to three consecutive state championships.) Coach Villers certainly made good on his investment. Either way, it didn't matter to me. Eric got what he needed and we survived the first day of school without parents. Take that, Texas sun.

15

Family Vacation

The last real family vacation I remember before George and Merle's passing was a trip to South Padre Island, Texas. George put us up in a beautiful hotel on the beach.

George and Merle wanted a day to themselves, so he gave Kurt his American Express Platinum Card and told him to go down to the waterfront and pay for an all all-day fishing trip. Like ducklings we fell in line and marched down to the waterfront, swimsuits, and towels in hand. Kurt found a lovely boat whose crew not only promised that everyone on board would catch a very large fish but that we'd also return with very full stomachs. This sounded good to us.

Shortly after, the vessel pushed from the docks and we were off on our fishing excursion with our very own Captain, first mate, and chef. The small crew was delighted to have four very happy children on their large boat and catered to our every desire. We ate lunch at tables adorned with beautiful white table clothes, crystal stemware, and as much caviar and as many virgin daiquiris as we wanted. It was a wonderful day and we returned to the hotel sun-kissed, happy, and exhausted.

We passed George and Merle outside the hotel; they were decked out in black tie on their way to a party. George asked us if we enjoyed our day, then told Kurt to order room service for dinner and watch movies in the room until they returned. I remember lying in bed that night thinking how truly fortunate I was to have such wonderful parents, even if they might be a tad crazy, and siblings who were so much fun. Around 2:00 AM I heard the adjoining door close and fell asleep feeling content, peaceful, and safe.

A couple of weeks after we returned from South Padre Island, Merle and the four of us were sitting in the family room watching *The Wonderful World of Disney*. It was a Sunday night tradition. George was at his desk paying bills.

"Sweet mother of Jesus!" George yelled, then busted into the center of the family room with a piece of paper gripped tightly in his hand and being erratically waived over his head. "Merle! What crazy person allows four children to rent a small yacht, complete with a staff for a day of deep sea fishing?"

The four of us kept focused on Tinker Bell flying across the screen. I wondered if I might need some of her fairy dust to fly away from this scene. Merle glided over to George and removed the bill from his clutch. She glanced at it quickly, looked at us for a moment, and then calmly stated, "The same crazy person who gives a 14-year-old a platinum American Express card and says go rent a boat for the day."

George nodded and returned to his desk. He grabbed his checkbook, took one more glance at the bill, looked Kurt dead in the eyes and said, "Always give a 20 percent tip Kurt, not 15," and then wrote the check.

Time waits for no one – life without George and Merle seemed to move quickly. Before I knew it, I was graduating from high school, my family, Kurt, Dana, and Eric, sitting in the auditorium watching as I walked across the stage. We all felt the relief that I had made it, but I would venture to say that Kurt and Dana felt it most. Together they had gotten me through school and Eric was on his way. George and Merle would have been proud.

After the ceremony, we went for a rare dinner out. On these occasions when we went out for burgers, the big discussion was whether we could afford the extra 20 cents for cheese. We were reluctant to spend money foolishly since it was so tight. Kurt always told Eric and me to get the cheese, but I never remember Kurt getting any. To this day, I have never seen Kurt eat a cheeseburger. Later that night, as I lay in my bed, I heard the all too familiar sound of the soup can hitting against my window. I reached inside and pulled out an encrypted note. It read, "Good job, I am proud of you. Love, Kurt." Tears fell from my eyes and I had no words to adequately express what I was feeling. I still don't.

Years later, while home on leave from the Army, I happened to drive past my childhood home. It was for sale and there was an open house. I parked out front and walked through our front door. The memories came flooding back and I smiled as I walked from room to room. I saw the notches on the trim where we recorded Eric's fast and furious growth spurts. I stood at the desk where George wrote the bills, and where I took over, out of necessity, the same job. I could still feel the love and warmth that permeated the home tucked in between the despair and hope. I didn't linger long... minutes maybe, but it felt like hours. I swore I saw George sitting at the desk, pacing in the trial room, Merle, her beautiful self, by his side. I was overcome with feelings that intertwined: Happiness, sadness, anger at George and Merle for having children when surely, they should have known that it would have been best had they just remained a couple in love. But I was also grateful. I was grateful for life, sweet childhood memories, my brothers and sister, and tender mercies. Part of me wanted to stay forever and recapture all that had happened inside these walls. I knew I could not and so I forced myself toward the front door. Another couple walked in just as I was about to leave. I turned to them and said, "Close the damn door."

The rule was that once you completed high school you were expected to be able to financially support yourself. I had saved almost all the money I made from my many jobs during the years and had enough for at least a semester at a state college. I joined my sister in Austin, Texas, where she was now attending the University of Texas Law School. She was delighted that we would be able to spend time together. I lasted two semesters at UT. I just couldn't work enough or sell enough plasma to support myself, so I decided I would join the military and save as much as possible. After four years, I would have enough to live and the Montgomery GI Bill would pay for school. Well, that was the plan at least. However, as you've read, things don't always go as planned. Not even "O" plans. Whether written or not.

I went to the recruiting station in Austin. All five services were represented in the same building. I started with the Navy because I liked the water and the thought of sailing around the world.

Unfortunately, I couldn't get past the bell-bottom pants.

Next.

The Marine recruiter was not very attentive to me; perhaps it was because I was five-foot two and barely 100 pounds. I'm pretty sure he didn't think I had what it took to be a Marine.

Next.

I didn't even bother talking to the Air Force recruiter because it held exactly zero appeal to me.

Next.

For no other reason that I can pinpoint, other than process of elimination, I turned to the Army. I tested high on the entrance exam and was deemed physically fit to serve. Soon after, I was on my way to basic training.

And that, my friends, is how it all started. Many of you reading this have your own stories of triumph and tragedy. It seems like in life, we all do. Of all that I know, one thing is certain, what doesn't kill you makes you stronger.

Strong.

Army Strong.

Made in USA - Kendallville, IN
1052164_9781984334954
11.04.2020 1426